FRAGILE
SUCCESS

FRAGILE SUCCESS

Nine Autistic Children, Childhood to Adulthood

by Virginia Walker Sperry

with a Foreword by Sally Provence, M.D.

ARCHON BOOKS
1995

First published 1995 as an Archon Book, an imprint of
The Shoe String Press, Inc., North Haven, Connecticut 06473.

Library of Congress Cataloging-in-Publication Data

Sperry, Virginia Walker, 1915–
    Fragile success: nine autistic children, childhood to adulthood /
by Virginia Walker Sperry; with a foreword by Sally Provence.
        p.   cm.
    Includes bibliographical references and index.
    ISBN 0-208-02413-1 (alk. paper)
    1. Autism in children—Case studies.   2. Autistic children.
I. Title.
RJ506.A9S68   1995
618.92'8982—dc20   95-14059
                                                              CIP

*All pictures and text in this book have been used by written
permission of the parents and/or guardians of the children
discussed, or the children themselves. The names of both
parents and children have been changed to protect their
privacy.*

The paper in this publication meets the minimum
requirements of American National Standard for Information
Science—Permanence of Paper for Printed Library Materials,
ANSI Z39.48—1984. ⊗

Designed by Abigail Johnston

Printed in the United States of America.

To Sally A. Provence, M.D.
September 4, 1916–February 6, 1993

*This book would not have been written without
her wisdom and guidance, and constant encouragement*

CONTENTS

FOREWORD

Fragile Success tells about the lives of people: about children who, when very young, were found to be very different from their peers in ways that perplexed and pained their parents and confounded their doctors and teachers; about how they changed, while remaining very much the same, over a time span of twenty-five years; about the philosophy, skill, warmth, and motivation of a dedicated teacher, Virginia Sperry, who has remained in touch with them and who knows them as adults. Through this book, Mrs. Sperry makes us very aware of the value of a teacher's knowing a child well and daring to be creative in using and modifying educational methods.

In the late 1950s, just before the children portrayed in this book were born, there were very few clinical or educational resources to serve autistic children and their parents and, indeed, few clinicians who recognized the characteristics that distinguished these children from those suffering from other severe childhood developmental and behavioral disorders. During the nearly forty intervening years, there have been hundreds of studies aimed at improving diagnosis and treatment of the group of clearly related disorders called by various names: infantile autism, childhood autism, infantile psychosis, childhood schizophrenia, atypical personality development, and, more recently, pervasive developmental disorder.

In their *Handbook of Autism and Pervasive Developmental Disorders*, editors D. J. Cohen and A. M. Donnellan

explain, "Those disorders were first described in the medical
literature only 40 years ago. Thirty years ago, treatment was
focussed almost exclusively on young children and consisted of
attempting to use psychotherapeutic techniques developed for
the therapy of neurotic children. Twenty years ago, behavioral
and educational interventions were initially attempted, bringing
along with them scientific interest in behavioral mechanisms.
Concurrently, neurochemical and other biomedical efforts were
initiated, and autism became conceptualized as a disorder re-
flecting abnormalities in brain maturation and function"
(p. xv).

The contrast between the 1950s and 1990s is worthy of
note. Now there is much greater understanding of the natural
history of the syndrome than there was in the 1950s. Parents
today, especially in the United States, England, and Canada, can
expect to find specialized diagnostic, treatment, and educational
programs. A child can now receive a detailed and comprehensive assessment of his or her intellectual and adaptive competence, and any associated medical conditions can be accurately
identified.

Currently too, there is agreement on the heterogeneity of
autism, that autism is not a single disease entity with a single
cause. Children diagnosed as autistic vary widely in intellectual
ability, adaptive and defensive capabilities, general level of
personality organization, and severity of symptoms.

The various chapters of this book show clearly the wisdom
of the teaching approach used by Mrs. Sperry in her years at
the Elizabeth Ives School for Special Children in New Haven,
Connecticut: that really to help a child learn how to cope with
the world, one must look for and nurture a child's strengths at
the same time as one attempts to alleviate his or her problems.
The statement of Mrs. Sperry's philosophy, the story of the
work at Ives School, and the individual case studies that follow
here make the reader vividly aware of how puzzling and hard

to reach and influence these children were, and of the patience and resourcefulness that was required of their teachers and therapists.

In addition to the case studies here, several parents have written about their children: about the emotional stress of caring for an autistic child; of the strain to which the families are subjected; of the long, hard road to understanding and acceptance. While there are unique features in the experiences of all families with autistic children, there are many shared ones: the search for answers and understanding; the feelings of despair and hope; the pain, anger, sadness, and frustration. To a greater or lesser extent, these all are a part of the experience of these families.

Particularly poignant are the accounts written by two mothers about their autistic daughters. Karen's mother's eloquent account covers twenty-five years and tells of the perplexity and pain as well as the efforts, successful and unsuccessful, she and the rest of the family have made to help Karen and to live with her day by day over the years. Polly's mother's story has a special vividness in the description of the effect Polly's problems have had and continue to have on the lives of her parents and brothers. By her own admission, Polly's mother is angry and embittered. She despairs of things ever being better for her and Polly. When asked if she had anything to add to her account, she said she did not, because "it hurts me too much to write any more about it." The other parental accounts show the possible variety of emotional reactions to having an autistic child, from gratitude and hopefulness to frustration and embitterment.

The nine case studies—Bill, David, Eric, Jimmy, Larry, Tom, John, Karen, and Polly—illustrate the similarities and differences of the syndrome in children who in early childhood would be considered moderately to severely dysfunctional. Through the stories set down in these pages, it is not difficult for the reader to identify how their parents and teachers experienced being with these children as they grew up. It is less easy to imagine the thoughts and feelings of the children/young adults themselves except at moments when their panic, fear, anger, or pleasure is apparent in their behavior. So though this book is about the children and their afflictions, it is also about the caring adults who, as parents and teachers, sought to understand, nurture, and help them.

Sally Provence, M.D.
Former Director,
Sally Provence-Irving B. Harris Child Development Center,
Yale University Child Study Center

ACKNOWLEDGMENTS

No words can fully express my gratitude to Sally Provence, M.D., Martha Leonard, M.D., and Mary McGarry, M.D. They gave me the benefit of their knowledge and skill in the field of autism and of early childhood development, and generously of their valuable time. I thank Fred R. Volkmar, M.D., and the talented professionals of the Child Development Unit (known now as the Sally Provence-Irving B. Harris Child Development Unit) of the Yale University Child Study Center, who throughout many years have contributed to this project—a project which often seemed to the author just a pipe dream.

Many friends, notably Sally H. Levinson, Rena Gans, Ann Bliss, M.S.W., Betty Sword, current director of Ives School, and former teachers of Ives were an invaluable help to me. Encouragement and input came from these professionals in the field of writing and editing: Mary Price; Gladys Topkis; Roberta Yerkes Blanshard; Richard Selzer, M.D.; Annabel Stehli; Maggie Scarf; Timothy Niederman; and my friends from college years, Alice Gore King, Phyllis Feldkamp, and Geraldine Rhoads.

My research took me to many private special education schools, and to special education departments of public school systems. The various professionals there were extraordinarily helpful either in discussing some of the children/young adults of this book, or in searching patiently for the appropriate files.

Starting in the mid-1970s, the parents of these children/

young adults have given me their cooperation and warm encouragement to persevere. I deeply appreciate their friendship
and their endurance of innumerable interviews and phone calls
required by the research for this book.

Sue Spight was instrumental in referring the manuscript to
my editor, Diantha Thorpe, who believed in *Fragile Success*. I
am indebted to her for her editorial skill and expertise which
shape this book, and to Sue Spight for her invaluable help.

INTRODUCTION

Thirty years ago, autism was a mysterious condition. It was poorly understood by physicians, and there was little concrete information available on its symptoms and treatment. From 1966 to 1972, the years that I was director of the Elizabeth Ives School for Special Children in New Haven, Connecticut, I often saw the painful frustration on the faces of the parents of the autistic children at the school as they endured the confusion and emotional turmoil that went with trying to cope with an autistic child.

Soon after my retirement in 1972, I ran into an eleven-year-old former Ives pupil and his mother in the aisle of a local supermarket. I had last seen the child when he was seven or eight. Sandy-haired, freckle-faced, and rangy in build, he beamed as he recognized me. Compared to the hyperactive, constantly chattering boy I had known, he seemed focused and in control. His mother told me proudly that her son was managing well in the special education program of his public school system. The change in him was really remarkable. She thanked me for the attention he had received at Ives, without which, she felt, he never would have come so far. In a flash of conviction and inspiration, it occurred to me that it could be beneficial to share with others, especially the parents of such children, some of the hard-won knowledge we at Ives had gained from working with autism.

Within a year, I began to collect data on the careers of

eleven graduates of Ives School. These children were chosen not because of their diagnosis but because I had a sound relationship with them and their parents. Geography defined the choice considerably, so they all lived within a manageable distance. Of the eleven, I have included nine stories of those whose original evaluation was "autistic," "autistic-like," or "personality disorder with autistic overlay."

The parents gave me permission to obtain information from the various institutions and programs that had treated their children. The Yale University Child Study Center in New Haven, Connecticut, which originally tested and diagnosed the nine children, provided facts on their early toddlerhood, doctors' and social workers' analyses, accounts, interviews, test scores, and final diagnoses. (Doctors at the Center's Child Development Unit, specifically Dr. Sally Provence, Dr. Martha Leonard, and Dr. Mary McGarry, referred their most puzzling younger children to the Ives School from the school's inception. These three particular doctors also became consultants for the school.) Other information came from records at nursery schools, public school special education programs, state-funded programs, and private special schools.

I compiled a full set of testing results for each child, from their earliest examinations through scores and grade-level achievements when each of the nine turned twenty-one and "graduated" from high school. To help complete the profiles, seven of the nine children were re-tested as adults at the Yale Child Study Center.

I interviewed the children's teachers, social workers, and parents, and as they got older I went to their graduations, their workshops, group homes, and places of work. I took many of the nine out to lunch several times and kept on interviewing them and their parents through 1989. At the time my research was complete, the children's ages ranged from twenty-three to thirty. My original goal of discovering how these nine children would develop as young adults had been accomplished. Nevertheless, although it is now 1995 and much time has passed since I completed my research, I still keep in touch with all of them.

The nine accounts in the following pages are the product of this work. It is now twenty-five years since these children, now adults, attended Ives, and the study and treatment of autism has broadened and developed so that the process they experienced as virtual pioneers—the programs for special children and the availability of special schools—is largely taken for granted. Readers may look on the description of these early years as a history of those who were among the first children to receive such special treatment. But the children of these nine stories are not history. Although they are now adults, and many have learned how to cope with their disability, their needs and characteristics have not changed. Nor has the problem of diagnosis been solved: There are still many children all over this country whose behavior, whether diagnosed autistic or atypical or even undiagnosed, confounds and disturbs their parents, doctors, and teachers. Such children present a challenge very similar to the challenge faced by those involved in the lives of the children in this book.

As the research grew, I questioned who would be the principal audience for this book. There were the pediatricians, who, in the early years of Ives, seemed largely unaware of childhood autism. Then there were the parents, fumbling, often despairing, and totally bewildered. They were constantly asking for guidance and reassurance, or at least some predictions as to the future. Other medical specialists and social workers, too, were baffled by these strange children. I wanted to address all three of these groups. During the 1960s and 1970s, we teachers of autistic youngsters were in a no-man's-land, where information, resources, and guidance were largely unavailable and where intuition and innovation were required daily tools of the trade. The book I wanted to achieve would record what we learned in an accessible manner so others—whether doctors, teachers, or parents—could benefit from it. This book also hopes to broaden the understanding of autism for various audiences, including employers and those in the community who deal with the autistic on a day-to-day basis. It is the kind of book I wish I had had when I taught at Ives School.

The subjects in this book are the young adults themselves from infancy to the present, their parents' experience of raising a developmentally disabled person, and the effect this had on the lives of parents and siblings. The following chapters will show who the very different autistic children are as adults, where they live, what work they can do, what deficits have been moderated, and what disabilities remain unchanged. These individuals are dramatic examples of the wide range of autistic behaviors, and their stories demonstrate the kind of parental interventions and the medical, educational, vocational, and recreational services that played an important part in their growing up.

There is a secondary theme and hypothesis to this book as well: Early, concentrated intervention has led to the achievement by these nine children of a comparative success in adulthood. Early diagnosis and medical and educational intervention saved each child. Without the unceasing dedication of parents, doctors, teachers, and other professionals, many, as adults, would be vegetating at home or in an institution. Like any other youngster, each of these children had talents that might well have been lost, totally blocked by their various handicaps. The effectiveness of our work at the Ives School was due largely to our firm belief that each child has his or her strengths and that, as with "normal" children, only by the discovery and use of their own individual talents can they really become strong and secure. Constant supportive guidance has helped all of the children in this book to use their talents and accomplish a limited or, in one and perhaps two cases, total independence.

To help the lay reader with the specialized terminologies of psychology and special education, I have *italicized* unfamiliar words and phrases in their first use and have defined them in the glossary. The children are most often referred to as "autistic children" or "autistics" here for clarity. Of course, by this I mean "children with autism." To obscure the identities of the children (and families) discussed, names and birthdates have been changed, and permission has been obtained for all material herein. The children, mothers, fathers, and siblings here stand as archetypes of the developmentally handicapped and their families across the country. The problems and solutions touched upon are universal.

I • CHILDHOOD AUTISM AND RELATED DISORDERS
by Sally Provence, M.D.

Childhood autism, the clinical diagnosis assigned to the children in this book, is not a single disease with a single cause: Children diagnosed as autistic vary widely in intellectual ability, adaptive and defensive capabilities, general level of personality organization, severity of symptoms, and the extent to which they improve over time.

The term *autism* (or *infantile autism*) was first used in 1943 by Dr. Leo Kanner, professor of psychiatry at the Johns Hopkins School of Medicine, to describe a severe disturbance in social relatedness appearing in very young children and characterized by a profound withdrawal from contact with others.[1] Associated with autism were the absence of speech or speech not intended for communication with others, an obsessive desire for sameness in the environment or pattern of the day, and panic reactions in which the child could not be comforted even by the best efforts of parents.

In the 1940s and 1950s, children with symptoms similar to Kanner's autism were given a wide variety of diagnoses, among them childhood schizophrenia, infantile psychosis, primary personality disorder, atypical personality development, and severe deviational development. By the early 1950s, when the Yale Child Study Center began its work with autistic and atypical children, there were two strongly divergent views about the cause of childhood psychoses, including autism. Many, citing Kanner's original report and the work of others such as L. Despert, and B. Rank, M. G. Putnam, and S. Kaplan, assumed that psychogenic factors, i.e., deficits or noxious influences in the environment, were the principal cause of the disorder. Others favored a biological explanation.

The theory of a psychogenic origin of autism predominated in the 1950s and early 1960s, when the children portrayed in this book were first diagnosed. This school of thought held that the roots of autism could be found in the particular parent–child relationship: A deviant relationship between parent and child, due to the emotional coldness of the parent, caused the child not to be able to relate to other people normally. This view stereotyped the parents, especially the mother, as "cold" (the "mathematician" father and "librarian" mother were typical images of "cold" parents of the time). The stereotype arose from Kanner's observation that certain parents were unable to provide a warm emotional environment, and that many of the collateral kin were strongly preoccupied with abstractions of a scientific, literary, or artistic nature, with limited interest in people. Despert's extensive work with disturbed parents of schizophrenic children and with the children themselves led her to propose the term "schizophrenogenic mother" or "frigid mother."[2] Putnam, Rank, and Kaplan reported a number of children with severe personality disorders whose mothers had been depressed or otherwise psychologically unavailable to them during infancy and introduced the term *atypical personality development* to characterize these children.[3]

In contrast to the theory of psychogenic origin was the position of L. Bender, and others, who believed the disorder to be of biological origin.[4] Kanner himself, in a follow-up study of children in his group published in 1971, attempted to clarify the misinterpretation of his theory, calling attention to a little-noted sentence in his original paper that stated that the children had been born with an innate inability to form the usual, biologically provided interest in people and social interchange.[5] He asserted that he did not assume a direct cause-and-effect relationship between parental personality characteristics and the autistic behavior of children.

Bender characterized autism as a childhood version of schizophrenia and based her conclusions on studies of more than 600 schizophrenic children between 1935 and 1952. Bender's definition went through various refinements and can be condensed as follows: Childhood schizophrenia (autism) is an emotional disturbance that reveals pathology in many areas of integration or patterning of the functions of the central nervous system. Interferences in normal developmental patterns and regressive reactions are common. Severe, overwhelming anxiety is a prominent feature. Secondary to anxiety are withdrawal from human contact; regressions in behavior or, in some, panic states; temper tantrums; phobias; fears; and compulsions.

In Bender's childhood schizophrenia, the child expresses profound difficulty and confusion about personal identity, body image, orientation in time and space, and human relationships. There are disturbances in movement, appearing both as variability in motor skill and as stereotyped, often peculiar-looking body movements. Some childhood schizophrenics exhibit early and late patterns of maturation, or retarded and precocious behavior, simultaneously.

Margaret Mahler, a psychiatrist at the New York Psychoanalytic Institute and another backer of the biological origin theory, referred to similarly disturbed children as psychotic and described autistic and *symbiotic* types with at least two features in common: alienation or withdrawal from reality and a severe

disturbance in the sense of self-identity.[6] Mahler's autistic type
is descriptively similar to Kanner's, but she looked on the
autism as the mechanism through which the child shuts out the
presumably unbearable sources of sensory stimuli in the outside
world, especially those that demand social–emotional response.
Mahler regarded symbiotic psychosis as a disturbance in the
interaction between mother and infant in which the infant does
not give clear signals of his or her needs and feeling states, and
where the mother may have serious deficiencies in her ability to
communicate with and nurture her infant.

Through the 1960s, the field of autism research and treatment was polarized by reports appearing to substantiate, or at
least to emphasize, one or the other of the theories of psychogenic or biological origin. Gradually the theories advocating a
totally psychogenic origin were discarded in favor of the practice of conducting diagnostic evaluations that included a careful
look at both physical and mental factors in the child as well
as conditions in the environment, particularly the family's
contribution toward aggravating or alleviating the child's disturbance. Clinics and child study centers undertook studies to
attempt to identify subgroups whose similarity might give clues
to more targeted and selective treatment: genetics; neurological
and neurochemical studies; methods of special education and
speech/communication therapy; behavioral adaptation of con-
ventional psychotherapy. Over time, a body of research has
appeared ranging from neurochemical research to trials of
various therapies and from cross-sectional examination to long-
term follow-up studies.[7]

It is now fairly widely accepted that "the social disabilities
of autistic persons are . . . recognized as a major if not *the*
major defining characteristic of the syndrome . . . however,
these factors have yet to be fully and adequately defined."[8] At
present, "the autistic disorders are best understood as compos-
ing part of a spectrum in which multiple and interacting influ-

ences—biological and environmental—determine both the severity of impairment and variations in its form within the syndrome."[9]

What has been discovered is the strong tendency in autistic children for certain features or behaviors to cluster together. These are: absence or severe impairment of two-way social interaction, nonverbal communication and imagination, and a pattern of activities dominated by stereotyped routines. These symptoms are, by and large, characteristic of all autistic children to one degree or another.

In 1987, Lorna Wing, M.D. of the Institute of Psychiatry and Anthony Attwood, Ph.D. of the Herefordshire Health Authority, both of England, suggested a clinically useful classification system to reduce some of the confusion engendered by the profusion of names of "new" syndromes that has arisen to describe the different combinations of features and behaviors exhibited by disturbed young children.[10] In this system, the major determinant of subclassification is the degree of impairment of social interaction. Autistic and atypical children are considered to belong to one of three groups: the "aloof" group, which consists of those who are most cut off from social contact; the "passive" group, which consists of those who do not make spontaneous social approaches except to obtain what they want or need; and the "active-but-odd" group, which consists of those who do make social approaches to others, but "in a peculiar, naive, and one-sided fashion."[11] This system does not totally solve the problem of classifying autistic disorders because of the variability in the additional findings in children in any one group (e.g., inborn errors of metabolism, lead encephalopathy, and other central nervous system disorders).

The characteristics exhibited by the aloof group are those that most commonly come to mind when the word *autism* is used; they correspond fairly closely to the behavior that Kanner originally observed and defined as infantile autism. Most members of this group are severely retarded, though a few may test in the normal or near-normal IQ range. Aloofness commonly appears as indifference to the presence or actions of others. In infants, this appears as an absence of normal attachment behavior. There is a lack of demonstration of affection or bids for comfort when distressed. Some individuals will initiate contact, but only as a means to obtaining a specific need, such as food; once the need is filled, the child abruptly moves away to be by itself again.

Characteristic of the aloof children is the lack of social communication, whether verbal or nonverbal. They will often not respond to direct speech and may appear deaf, except that they will react to other sounds that have meaning for them, such as a refrigerator door opening, a car driving by, etc. Aloof children who do speak often have a monotonous or otherwise abnormal voice quality and tend to exhibit other speech abnormalities such as *echolalia* (repetition of a phrase or sentence spoken by another person), pronoun reversal, excessive literalness in usage, and use of the minimum number of words necessary to carry meaning. Most important, aloof children do not use speech to communicate in the sense of an exchange for pleasure or comparison of ideas or interests. Speech is merely a tool to satisfy the individual's particular and immediate needs.

Aloof children tend to lack the capacity for imaginative play, although some may have highly developed manipulative skills. Instead of imaginative play, an aloof child may perform a single repetitive, stereotyped activity, and remain totally absorbed in that activity for hours on end. A child's attachment to one particular activity may persist for days or even years, until another similar activity takes its place. To a certain extent, a child's level of intelligence will affect the nature of this type of activity as the child gets older. Children of low intelligence will continue to perform simple activities, such as flapping their arms or rocking or other simple body movements. More capable children can, as they age, exhibit more complex repetitive behavior in the form of collecting objects or creating involved, rigid patterns of personal behavior, such as needing to take the same route to the store every time or needing to put clothes on in a certain order.

Wing and Attwood's second category, the passive group, tends to have a higher level of ability than the aloof group and to perform better on visuospatial tasks than in verbal skills. Members of this group with intelligence in the normal range can often manage in public school. Like those in the aloof group, members of this group tend not to make spontaneous social contact, but in general may be approached without resistance and may be led in games, although they are likely to remain in a passive role.

Although the facility for speech is better developed in members of the passive group than in the aloof group, it still shows the same sort of abnormalities. The main difference between the passive group and the aloof group is that, although members exhibit many of the same behaviors, the behaviors are less marked in the passive group. Because of their ability to respond to others, members of this group are often not diagnosed until they reach school age.

The third group, the active-but-odd group, possesses many of the abnormalities in language and behavior of the other two groups, with the major distinction of being able to initiate contact with other people, though in oddly mannered ways. The contact is still not for real engagement and may be so persistent as to be disturbing to the person addressed. Many children in this group speak late, although some, when they do begin to speak, are able immediately to use complete sentences and long words. Speech is still repetitive, long-winded, unnaturally formal, and over-literal. Nonverbal communication, interestingly, tends also to be impaired in this group with excessive or absent eye contact, odd or absent inflection, and odd body movements during conversation.

Active-but-odd children display characteristic autistic behaviors but may have more pronounced behavioral problems than passive and aloof children. Older active-but-odd children in particular may get into trouble through socially inappropriate behavior in public. Like the passive group, active-but-odd children are often not diagnosed until they are of school age.

There are ongoing efforts to develop systems of classifying the developmental and psychiatric disorders of infancy and early childhood based on research and accumulating experience with a variety of diagnostic and treatment methods. There is still much to be learned before the various disorders can be clearly distinguished from each other.

It was recognized in the 1950s at the Yale Child Study Center and other clinics that a comprehensive approach to understanding the child was necessary. Physical and neurological examinations, hearing tests, and laboratory tests for inborn errors of metabolism and other biochemical aberrations, though less refined than now, were much utilized by referring physicians and the clinic staff. Developmental and psychometric tests were part of the evaluation, as were play sessions with the child. It was usually difficult or impossible to perform complete standardized psychometric tests and arrive at an intelligence quotient (IQ score) with meaning because of the unresponsiveness of the child or his or her inability to undertake the tasks. What one could usually do was to establish levels of functioning in various domains of development (e.g., motor skills, nonverbal problem-solving, speech, social behavior, play behavior, etc.), and this, combined with the always valuable information from parents, permitted a synthesis of findings.

In the early childhood years, based on the functional and behavioral picture presented by the child, it is possible to classify autistic children as mildly, moderately, or severely disturbed, and to plan treatment accordingly. Nevertheless, this does not warrant a long-term prediction about the future development for an individual child, even though, as a group, most autistic children retain a degree of impairment ranging from relatively mild to severe.

As the case studies in this book illustrate, preschool-year global IQ scores often either cannot be established or are of no value in reaching a diagnosis. Marked scatter in test performance is common, and variations in symptoms and abilities are often extreme. Islets of unusual ability exist alongside deficits in abstract thinking. Some children show remarkable musical, drawing, or sculpting abilities. Others demonstrate astonishing feats of memory or excel in such activities as block design and details of maps or subway systems. Beyond the difficulty in understanding these special abilities, such feats add to parents' perplexity about their child. In such instances, the social dysfunction and the major disturbances in communication—language as well as social communication—remain central and defining features of autistic disorders.

Given the severity of the conditions, their perplexing nature, and the relatively poor prognosis, it is not surprising that many treatments have been utilized.[12] Behavioral modification procedures may be helpful in increasing appropriate and decreasing inappropriate behavior. Psychotherapy is suitable only for a small percentage of autistic individuals. Medications, though they have not proved to be curative, may have a limited role in management of certain cases.

As Dr. Fred Volkmar of the Yale Child Study Center has indicated, the best available evidence at present suggests that early and continuous intervention is highly desirable—appropriate educational interventions to foster acquisition of basic social, communicative, and cognitive skills.[13] Another very important development has been the realization in the professional community that not only must professionals in-form parents of the need, over the long term, to be advocates for their autistic children in a variety of social and administrative settings, but that professionals must also be prepared to assist parents in this advocacy.

NOTES

1. See L. Kanner, "Autistic Disturbances of Affective Contact," *Nervous Child* 2 (1943): 217–50.

2. L. Despert, "Some Considerations Relating to the Genesis of Autistic Behavior in Children," *American Journal of Orthopsychiatry* 21 (1951): 335–50; M.G. Putnam, B. Rank, E. Pavenstedt, E.N. Anderson, and I. Rawson, "Round Table, 1974, Case Study of an A-Typical Two-and-a-Half-Year-Old," *American Journal of Orthopsychiatry* 18 (1948): 1–30; M.G. Putnam, B. Rank, and S. Kaplan, "Notes on John I.: A case of primal depression in an infant," in *Psychoanalytic Study of the Child*, vol. 6 (New York: International Universities Press, 1951), 49–51; B. Rank, "Intensive Study and Treatment of Pre-School Children Who Show Marked Personality Deviations of 'A-Typical Development' and Their Parents," in *Emotional Problems of Early Childhood* (New York: Basic Books, 1955), 491–501.

3. M.G. Putnam et al., "Notes on John I.," 49–51.

4. L. Bender, "Childhood Schizophrenia: A Clinical Study of 100 Schizophrenic Children," *American Journal of Orthopsychiatry* 17 (1947): 40–56; L. Bender, "Schizophrenia in Childhood: Its Recognition, Description and Treatment," *American Journal of Orthopsychiatry* 26(3) (1956): 499–506.

5. L. Kanner, "Follow-up Study of Eleven Autistic Children Originally Reported in 1943," *Journal of Autism and Childhood Schizophrenia* (1971): 1, 119–145.

6. M. Mahler, "On Childhood Psychosis and Schizophrenia: Autistic and Symbiotic Infantile Psychoses," in *Psychoanalytic Study of the Child*, vol. 7 (New York: International Universities Press, 1952), 280–94; M. Mahler, *Our Human Symbioses and the*

Vicissitudes of Individuation (New York: International Universities Press, 1968).

7. The Yale Child Study Center, to name one, has produced for over forty years a variety of research papers and clinical studies on autistic and atypical children. See, e.g., S. Ritvo and S. Provence, "Form Perception and Imitation in Some Autistic Children: Diagnostic Findings and Their Contextual Interpretation," in *Psychoanalytic Study of the Child*, vol. 8 (New York: International Universities Press, 1953); D.J. Cohen, B.K. Caparulo, B.A. Shaguritz, and M.B.J. Bowers, "Dopamine and Serotonin Metabolism in Neuropsychiatrically Disturbed Children: CSF Homovanillic Acid and 5-hydroxyindolacetic Acid," *Archives of General Psychiatry* 34 (1977): 545–50; B.K. Caparulo and D.J. Cohen, "Developmental Language Disorders in the Neuropsychiatric Disorders of Childhood," in K.E. Nelson, ed., *Children's Language* (New York: Gardner Press, 1983); F.R. Volkmar, D.M. Stier, and D.J. Cohen, "Age of Onset of Pervasive Developmental Disorder," *American Journal of Psychiatry* 142 (1985): 1450–52; E.K. Dahl, D.J. Cohen, and S. Provence, "Developmental Disorders Evaluated in Early Childhood: Clinical and Multivariate Approaches to Nosology of PDD," *Journal of the American Academy of Child Psychiatry* 25 (1986): 170–80; S. Sparrow, L.A. Rescorlo, S. Provence, S. Condon, D. Goudreau, and D. Cicchetti, "Mild Atypical Children—Preschool and Follow-up," *Journal of the American Academy of Child Psychiatry* 26 (1986): 181–85; S. Provence and E.K. Dahl, "Disorders of Atypical Development: Diagnostic Issues Raised by a Spectrum Disorder," in D.J. Cohen and A.M. Donnellan, eds., *Handbook of Autism and Pervasive Developmental Disorders* (New York: John Wiley & Sons, 1987) [hereinafter cited as Cohen & Donnellan], 155–61; F.R. Volkmar, "Social Development," Cohen & Donnellan, 41–60. See generally Cohen & Donnellan.

8. F.R. Volkmar, "Social Development," Cohen & Donnellan, 55.

9. S. Provence and E.K. Dahl, "Disorders of Atypical Development: Diagnostic Issues Raised by a Spectrum Disorder," Cohen & Donnellan, 677.

10. L. Wing and A. Attwood, "Syndromes of Autism and Atypical Development," Cohen & Donnellan, 3.

11. Ibid., 9.

12. F.R. Volkmar, "Autism and Pervasive Developmental Disorders," in M. Lewis, ed., *Child and Adolescent Psychiatry: A Comprehensive Textbook* (1991), 505.

13. Ibid., 499–507.

II • TEACHING THE AUTISTIC CHILD: THE WORLD OF THE IVES SCHOOL

T he children who are the subjects of the case studies to follow all attended the Elizabeth Ives School for Special Children in New Haven, Connecticut, between 1963 and 1972. All came to the school as preschoolers after being diagnosed autistic or autistic-like at the Yale Child Study Center in New Haven.

Well into the 1950s, American public education systems were not equipped to handle children whose educational needs differed greatly from those of the general school population. Consequently, physically, emotionally, and mentally handicapped children were often regarded as unteachable. One of the first people in the United States to assert that the public must take responsibility for the care and education of retarded and developmentally handicapped children was Dr. Arnold Gesell, a founder of the Clinic of Child Development, now known as the Yale Child Study Center, who crusaded for public understanding and acceptance of such abnormal conditions in children as minimal brain disorder, mental subnormality, convulsive seizure disorders, autism, and infant psychoses.[1] From 1913 through the 1950s, he campaigned for intelligence tests,

public school special education classes, special education training for teachers, and, especially, developmental testing of infants in order to permit early diagnosis by pediatricians and
psychologists.

Nevertheless, by the mid-1950s there were still only isolated responses to the needs of developmentally handicapped
children in the United States. Notable exceptions were the
demonstration-pilot study on the education of hyperactive and
brain-injured children at the Montgomery County Public
School System in Rockville, Maryland,[2] and the day-treatment
center pioneered by Carl Fenichel at the League School for
Seriously Disturbed Children in Brooklyn, New York.

The dearth of services for small children who were autistic,
autistic-like, or otherwise developmentally handicapped was
typical not only of the United States but of England and Europe
as well. Organizations in Europe and the United States that
treated autistic children were typically child study centers, child
development centers, or nursery schools for young children
who were deaf, blind, crippled, cerebral-palsied or retarded,
where developmentally handicapped children were often
lumped together with the mentally retarded.

In the 1950s to mid-1960s, several organizations in England and Canada were among the first to pioneer educational
methods for emotional and developmental handicaps different
from mental retardation or mental deficiency. Among these
were the West End Crèche in Toronto, Canada, and, in England,
the Clinic at Smith Hospital at Henley-on-Thames; the High-
wick Psychiatric Unit in St. Albans; and the Abingdon Child
Guidance Clinic and the Tesdale School, both in Abingdon.[3]
These schools within hospitals or clinics were the prototypes of
schools for autistic children, and wherever one existed, it became the springboard from which separate nursery schools,
kindergartens, and public school classes came into being.

The Ealing School, one of the first English schools, was described thus:

> The Society for Autistic Children has opened a school at Ealing, the administrative arrangements of which have proved most satisfactory so that I will take them as a convenient model. The premises were purchased and adapted by funds raised by the Society. The salaries and training costs were met from fees paid by the local authorities, but it is likely that there will be a deficiency each year to be covered by voluntary contributions. The school is open for the usual three terms a year. The hours are 9:30 A.M. to 4 P.M. . . . At the outset there were ten children, most of whom I had previously taught in another school .
> . . . There were 8 boys and two girls. More girls would have been accepted, but the applications were almost all for boys.[4]

The description of the Ealing School (with the exception of the financing) fits the Ives School at its inception.

In 1963, before the Ives School was founded, there was in the New Haven area no school for preschool-aged autistic, atypical, or severely developmentally disabled children. A special nursery school at the Yale Child Study Center took preschool children with developmental disabilities. One other private school took special children, but at the elementary level only. To address this need, Elizabeth Ives, a teacher of neurologically impaired children, started what later became the Ives School in two Sunday school rooms at the church where her husband was minister. Together with doctors from the Yale Child Study Center and several parents whose children were being seen there, Mrs. Ives developed a preschool program for young, developmentally disabled children. Ives's program became a pioneer in the field of education for the autistic preschooler.

Mrs. Ives died suddenly within a year after the founding of the school. The parents, doctors, and educators involved with the school elected to continue its work and reorganized the school under a new director and under the new name of the "Elizabeth Ives School for Special Children."

After two years, the school enlarged from five teachers and ten children to eight teachers and fourteen children. Most of the children were referred to Ives through the Yale Child Study Center and other child development clinics. A few came from psychiatrists in private practice, and one or two were referred directly from public school systems. In 1965 and 1966, two other private schools for developmentally disabled children were started in the community. One of these schools was for the severely autistic, those who would now be diagnosed as having pervasive development disorder. The other school was designed to educate older children and adolescents with a variety of moderate to severe developmental disabilities.

The Ives School was set up in the church much like any other preschool. The two upstairs Sunday school rooms were equipped like nursery school rooms, with corners for doll play and block play and painting and listening to music, and a place for books where children could sit and look at pictures. In each room there was a completely equipped play kitchen, which was very popular, and a place for water play. Various other centers of interest were set up around the room with dividers, creating cozy places where these often distractible, often hyperactive children could find privacy and quiet. As the school grew, it expanded to rooms in the church's basement. One room was used for one-to-one teaching or to separate an unruly child from the group. (Some of the children called this room "the jail.")

The church also had a large, sunny playground equipped with climbing bars, seesaw, a variety of sizes of swings and a glider swing, a sandpile, and various sizes of trucks and tricycles. Each spring, the faculty put together an order for new toys, games, and other teaching tools for the following September. There was also a large gymnasium in the church's basement, which was used often, particularly on rainy days. As the teachers' awareness of the children's needs grew, they began to use the gymnasium at the church more and added a swimming program in coordination with the YWCA. (This was particularly valuable for those children who needed to gain a better sense of their bodies.) The school hired a social worker (principally to work with parents), a speech therapist, and a physical education teacher. The faculty also began meeting on a biweekly basis with referring doctors who were specialists in the field of autism. Each of those sessions was devoted to a single child. Consulting with someone who was clinically trained and not involved with the children and was very supportive and helped increase the faculty's knowledge of autism and expertise in teaching the children.

The administrative setup of the Ives School was informal. Faculty meetings were held on Friday afternoons. They were group cooperatives in which the teachers collectively discussed schedules, new activities, needed changes, and teaching techniques for one child or another. Faculty meetings were not only a means of planning programs and future curriculum, but were vitally important for mutual support. The teachers listened to each other's problems, discouragements, and sometimes moans of utter exhaustion. The collective sympathy, suggestions on "how to," and praise for each other's successes saw the staff through many difficult periods.

A board made up of the doctors, several interested members of the church in which the Ives School was lodged, parents, and the director was responsible for the business side of the school. Tuition at Ives was low, $400 yearly, largely because in the mid-1960s parents had to pay for their own child. Consequently, salaries were also comparatively low, approximately $1,200 to $1,800 a year. With the passage of the

Elementary and Secondary Education Act of 1965, and the amendment to this act in 1966, the financial aspect of the school improved. The Elementary and Secondary Education Act provided for federal assistance for programs to educate low-income handicapped children, and the amendment to it created a Bureau for the Education of the Handicapped. This meant that the public school systems began to pay tuition for children attending schools such as Ives.

Children were referred to the Ives School from many sources: individual psychiatrists, pediatricians, general practitioners, and developmental pediatric specialists, as well as child development and pediatric clinics. Usually, a doctor or staff person contacted the director of Ives about a particular child, after which, with parental permission, the director and sometimes other staffers at Ives observed the child at play. They discussed the child's condition with the referring individuals and then decided if the Ives program was appropriate. Once Ives tentatively accepted the child, the parents came in to be interviewed. These admission interviews were held in the spring, and if all went well, the child entered the Ives program the next fall. Before the child came, all relevant material on him or her was forwarded to Ives from the referring source, and Ives staffers met with the child's social workers, teachers, and doctors. This helped the Ives people obtain enough understanding of the particular child to prepare a tentative individualized program.

The schedule at Ives was 8:30 A.M. to 2 P.M., Monday through Thursday. Because of the Friday afternoon faculty meetings, Friday was a short day, 9 A.M. to noon, and was totally taken up with the swimming program. When the children arrived each day, they hung up their coats and played for a while with whatever interested them. This was the settling-down period; it took about a half-hour. Then came a work period. In the beginning, one teacher conducted the work period for several children while the other teacher supervised the remaining children at play. As the children adjusted to the routine and their behavior improved, each of the two teachers in the room was able to work with a child on a one-to-one basis while the other two or three children played.

Work period covered areas of specific needs. Given the children's different kinds of developmental disabilities in perception, eye-hand coordination, language and speech, and motor control, the teaching was tailored to meet each child's deficits, using strengths to help weaknesses, not "drilling" addressed to the deficits.

After the work period, there were games or some sort of collective activity, such as story reading, that got the children together and gave them the feeling of being part of a group. Then there was a juice break. Afterward, weather permitting, there was outside play. There sometimes were trips and walks in a nearby park where there were slides, swings, and a sandpile.

Each teacher at Ives kept day-to-day records on each child in individual notebooks. Important as it is to keep an account of a child's progress in a regular classroom, it was an absolute necessity to keep written notes on these children. There were no published guidelines for teaching autistic children, and no previous experience had prepared the teachers to handle their puzzling, sometimes shocking behavior. The teachers were therefore actually creating entirely new teaching strategies. Recording the specific instances of what had worked or not worked with one child helped teachers plan for that child's future and also permitted new techniques to be generalized or adapted to activities for other children. These notebooks offered an invaluable backlog of information. It was one of the ways the teachers at Ives learned how to teach atypical children, at least in the first two years. Later, the school shifted to more efficient record-keeping.

Ives was a preschool only and stopped at the first- to

second-grade level. Depending on the severity of their impairment, the children went from Ives to one of four or five external programs. The choice was the combined decision of the child's parents, their consulting physician, the director of the Ives School, a representative of the proposed school, and, after the public schools were required to provide funding, the child's public school social worker. Several of the most severely impaired, many of whom were nonverbal, went to a private program for such children. Some students went to another private school that took them through the equivalent of high school. A few were able to go to regular classes at public school. A majority "graduated" into special education programs for the developmentally handicapped at public schools.

Legislation in 1966 had required Connecticut public schools to offer more varied classes for children with developmental disabilities. Programs, termed "service centers," were started under Connecticut Statute 10-66 and included a communication disorders program for autistic and autistic-like children. Children from Ives most often went to either the program for communication disorders or other types of special education classes.

The Children: Perplexed and Perplexing

The children admitted to the Ives School were between the ages of three and six to seven years old, and all had been diagnosed as autistic-like or atypical. They were impaired in their speech and understanding of language, and many were nonverbal or minimally verbal. Many had severe perceptual-motor and eye-hand control problems. Hyperactive, sometimes violent, sometimes withdrawn, they were considered ineducable. They had been excluded from normal nursery schools and frequently from special education services in the public schools.

When they arrived at Ives, all of the children had the air

of being lost, with little sense of self. Most of them had no idea which side of their body was left or right; sometimes they seemed to have no understanding that they had a body at all. Many had compulsive, self-stimulating, stereotypic gestures such as aimless hand flailing, jumping up and down, turning one hand back and forth and looking at it as if mesmerized, walking on tiptoe, whirling around, and darting aimlessly about. A few ran headlong, usually out the door into the church hallways and once or twice even out into the street.

Wild, disoriented behavior; sudden, violent temper tantrums or hysterical crying spells; and catastrophic reactions to another child or to a change or to nothing readily identifiable—all were typical. A child might be intelligent and able to relate comparatively well to people and the environment and yet be subject to sudden, violent outbursts—screaming; racing around the room destroying everything; grabbing a teacher and mouthing or biting arms, shoulders, or breasts; swearing repetitively; or running out of the classroom.

Some were too quiet, and most of them seemed remote and unreachable. One little boy, new to the school, chose to sit in a chair, isolated in the middle of the room. He held himself together with such tension, staring as through a fog, that he gave the impression of total fragility. All of the children projected fearfulness, varying from remoteness to shyness, and to anxiety sometimes amounting to panic. They often felt acute or chronic discomfort in situations most young children would consider manageable or even interesting. Very seldom did any child exhibit signs of pleasure or enjoyment.

The children's expressions of their fearfulness were often peculiar. One child would back into the room with his eyes covered by his arm and seat himself by backing up to a chair. He was never seen to miss. Another walked around with his eyes covered most of the time, one eye peeking under his arm. Many refused to look at others or seemed to look through them as though they did not exist. One child needed to hide in his teacher's coat when they went on walks. It took weeks for him to gather the courage to come out from under it.

The children very rarely used speech in social communication. Their speech was characterized by a variety of verbal expression: babbling interspersed with meaningless shouts; superficial glibness interrupted by sudden hysterical crying and screaming; illogical nonstop chatter; swearing; loud, fast repetition of words; echolalia; speaking with a rising inflection so that every sentence sounds like a question; or using only three or four words as a sort of chant. Two of the greatest challenges the teachers at Ives faced were to discern what was behind the speech these children did use, and to get them to speak meaningfully.

The most common and distinguishing characteristic of all these children was what one referring physician called their "imperviousness": that air of remoteness each displayed toward others. Each acted as though an invisible wall existed between him or her and everyone else. All of the children tended to treat other people, including their teachers, as objects of function only, as beings without recognizable personality. One little boy spent much of his time whirling aimlessly around the room. When he wanted to go from one room to the other, he would take his teacher's hand, place it on the doorknob, and twist the hand as a signal that he wanted to open the door. To him, the teacher was nothing more than a tool, some kind of human can-opener.

Their inability to relate normally to others in no way meant that these children were unaware of their surroundings, however. One child who constantly stared ahead was given a demonstration by a teacher of how to do a three-piece puzzle. The teacher left the three pieces on the side for him to place. The child did not even look at the pieces, but when the teacher turned away momentarily, he did the puzzle in a flash—

correctly. When the teacher turned around to look at him, he was again staring at the wall.

The Teaching Method at the Ives School

In the early 1950s, several therapies emerged aimed at developmentally handicapped children. There was the method of play therapy advocated by Dr. Virginia Mae Axline of the School of Education at New York University, a student of "nondirective" therapist Dr. Carl Rogers; the system of behavioral modification developed by Harvard psychologist B.F. Skinner, which is currently used by many schools; and the theory of muscular basis of behavior expounded by Newell C. Kephart, of Purdue University's department of psychology.[5] In addition, many special education classes in both private and public schools incorporated ideas on spatial orientation put forward by Dr. Ray Barsch, Professor of Special Education at Southern Connecticut State College.[6]

The underlying philosophy of school founder Elizabeth Ives was based on the work of Syracuse University department of education's William M. Cruickshank.[7] Ives used handmade teaching materials: red, blue, green, and yellow squares, triangles, and circles; block pattern designs, going on to pictures of increasingly difficult block structures; pegboard patterns made with dots on tagboard to be copied by the child on the child's own pegboard; and two-, three-, and four-piece puzzles, usually magazine pictures cut in halves or thirds and mounted. Her method was an individualized, slowed-down, concrete form of teaching.

Teaching an Autistic Child

The Ives preschool represented an effort to approximate as closely as possible regular nursery-school-through-first-grade programs and techniques. The curriculum and instructional materials were directed toward the specific perceptual, language, and comprehension deficits of the children. There was strong emphasis on social interaction and language and on the educational function of play, interwoven with some special education techniques.

Throughout the school day, there was attention to language. The children had an acute need for inner, expressive, and receptive language. They were asked to perform basic exercises such as naming objects, then pictures, then telling a simple, one-sentence story from a picture. The teachers also used puppetry, acting out nursery rhymes, creative rhythms to music, and nonobjective painting. Everything the children did—outdoor play, games, trips, walks to the park—contributed in some way to purposeful language development.

To enable the children to name their feelings, teachers often started with simple pictures, naming them "sad," "happy," or "angry." Eventually the child was able to make a happy face or a sad face and would be shown his happy or sad face in a mirror. Teachers interpreted other children's feelings for the child he or she was working with. The teachers also tried to get the children to realize and articulate their own feelings. A teacher would say to a child who had become remote or who was distracted, "Tell me what you are thinking. It will help you keep your mind on your work."

There were also games: the hokey-pokey, "Here We Go 'Round the Mulberry Bush," blind-man's buff, hide and seek, and "I Spy." Each one taught directionality, coordination, and how to be with a group. Each involved the child's seeing himself or herself as a person. Games also taught the children how to have fun, an unusual experience for most of them.

Of particular use were mirrors, tape recorders, puppets, and telephones. These tools, perhaps because of their impersonality, were very successful in teaching autistic children. Each one allowed the children to distance themselves from direct, face-to-face personal contact. One child, usually out of touch with people around him, talked freely on the telephone. Another, in the course of being retested as an adult, made his highest score answering questions over the telephone.

The school's puppet theater functioned similarly. A real-looking stage with a backdrop, it stood on a table that was tall enough so first-graders could stand up behind it and yet be hidden by curtain-skirts. Making scenery and furniture enchanted the children, and the impersonality of the theater encouraged them to talk.

Some children needed a great deal of time and repetition to grasp things. For example, the children played a game called "Postman" using flash cards of beginning reading vocabulary and their own names. One child was the postman. Another stood and asked, "Good morning. Do you have a letter for me?" The postman was supposed to reply, "What's your name?" and the other child would say his or her name. But one boy, when he was postman, parroted the other child by repeating, "Good morning. Do you have a letter for me?" The teacher would have to lead him though the game and get him to repeat "What's your name?" after her. It took two months of endless drill for the boy to cease echoing and ask "What's your name?" on his own.

The teachers worked on each child's body image in a variety of ways: naming the parts on a doll and matching these to the arms, legs, and other parts of the child's own body; using full-length mirrors; using paper dolls and pictures; and having the child crawl under or over a broomstick. Playing outdoors on the climber, seesaw, and glider swing, using a walking board, and swimming all improved body image also.

Nearly all the children had perceptual confusions or problems of identifying objects and perceiving them in space. The difficulty with spatial relationships, part of the general perceptual deficit, was compounded by the children's general lack of a sense of their own bodies and self. To address perceptual problems, teachers first used real objects, later going to worksheets and pencil-and-paper exercises. Once the children could identify an object and its position in space, they were made to understand and distinguish "in front of," "in back of," "beside," "above," "below," and so on.

The children also had difficulty with perceptual constancy, the ability to recognize shapes consistently (circle, triangle, square, and, later, oblong), not just in their simple forms but in other representations as well. The children learned the word "circle" along with the concept of "circleness." As a first exercise, they were to sort circles, squares, and triangles, at first by color and then by shape. This exercise was simple and unthreatening, and most of the children were willing to try it. (The ability to do this is part of normal public school first-grade reading readiness.) The perceptual constancy exercises progressed to where the children had to find a square in a house, a triangle in a sail or a tree, and so on.

Many of the children also had figure-ground problems: They were unable to distinguish foreground from background, auditorily or visually. This problem showed in the distractibility of the children; everything within their line of vision or hearing had equal importance to them. They needed training to be able to focus on one or two elements and block out the rest. Auditory figure-ground exercises were done with the speech therapist as well as with the teachers.

Often the children had deficiencies in their visual-motor skills, i.e., the coordination of vision with muscular movement and control, sometimes called eye-hand control. Many could not draw a line on the chalkboard from the edge to a chalk dot in the middle or could not balance blocks. Or if they could balance blocks, they could not balance the blocks in a pattern to make a block structure.

Even when they understood spatial ideas, severe perceptual motor problems sometimes made it difficult for them to put one block "on top of" another. Some could not identify shapes or textures by touch, could not cut with scissors following a line, or use a stencil. They often could not cut shapes in paper or put paste on a pre-cut piece of paper. One child was twenty-one years old before she could cut out a valentine! Visual-motor difficulties had little or nothing to do with mental impairment, however, and often the more mentally deficient of the children demonstrated good coordination in fine-motor skills. Because of the absence of firm guidelines for dealing with the problems of these children, much of what the teachers did was necessarily intuitive, but this quite often turned into successful teaching. One child, for instance, could not separate from his mother. He had spent the first two years of his life apart from his mother, mostly in the hospital. In school, the minute she moved one inch away from him, he would honk with alarm like a baby elephant. Realizing the depth of his panic, the teacher decided to try separating the two very slowly. The mother first sat right next to him and then very slowly, under his teacher's instructions, inched her chair backwards day by day. It took a whole month for her to get from the play table, where he was playing, back to the wall of the room, but by that time he paid hardly any attention to the fact that his mother was not near him. The day of success came when, at the time for outdoor play, he got up and ran out of the room with the other children into the play yard without a backward glance at his mother. He had learned to leave her himself, certainly, but he had also been taught.

Successful teaching, of course, is relative. At Ives, each child had his or her own special teacher. The success of the teaching depended on the establishment of a consistent, unbroken relationship between child and teacher. For example, in using a color-matching exercise with an inattentive, withdrawn, or hyperactive young boy, the teacher might put down a red square, saying "red," and one blue square, saying "blue," and then carefully and slowly hand a blue cardboard square to the child. The color would catch the child's attention, and he would match it with the blue square. The teacher might have to say, "Where does this go? Blue goes on blue," or show him once. If the child performed the exercise successfully, it meant that his awareness had been captured and he had focused on the exercise, if only for a few seconds. This was the equivalent of getting a foot in a door. Then the door could be pried farther open. The child's attention span could be stretched, under patient teaching, from seconds to minutes, with the child receiving constant praise from the teacher. As the child felt successful, he or she became less hyperactive, less withdrawn, and more attentive.

Successfully Teaching the Autistic

The educational approach required for these children, and the goals that the Ives School's faculty tried to achieve in teaching each child, were summed up by a referring specialist with regard to one little boy, Louis:

> Louis is asking for a world that will control, limit, and organize him since he is not able to do it for himself. He seeks an environment that recognizes his difficulty in screening stimuli, in focusing in on a particular one. His need to control others, his discomfort with answers that only lead to more questions, his compulsive need to destroy things are calls for help in the fragile world in which he attempts to function.

To break through to an autistic child, teaching must be patient, unrelenting, and caring, to enable the child to become engaged in learning and with people. This was the basic approach of teachers at Ives. The teaching at Ives was also

informed: It was founded on sound knowledge of child development and general early childhood and elementary school educational techniques, and it was augmented by skilled medical and
social work consultants.

But despite the improvements in teaching children with
educational special needs since Ives was founded, the basic
truth remains that teaching these and other children with special
needs is a demanding, strenuous, and often frustrating job.
Teachers are regularly exhausted, drained of energy at the end
of the day. They are sometimes bitten, kicked, or slapped, and
are often put in awkward and embarrassing positions. One
middle-aged teacher at Ives was thrown onto the sidewalk and
sat on by one of the larger Ives children who had exploded in a
sudden temper tantrum. The teacher was only able to get up
when a teenager from a local high school happened by and
lifted the child off her.

For those who work in this field, it is true that a thirty-
second breakthrough, the smallest lightning-flash of victory,
counterbalances the exhaustion and sends the teacher home in
a glow of success. Those who are committed to these children
find this is reward enough. Physical endurance, emotional stability, flexible responses, ability and willingness to improvise,
and an intuitive "gut" feeling about a child—all of these are
needed to work with developmental disabilities.

This kind of teaching is not everyone's cup of tea. Between
1966 and 1972, three people at Ives were counseled to leave
the field, one because she was afraid of physical violence and
two others because they wanted "organized" classrooms. The
Ives School staff evolved into a unique group of caring and
informed people, each of whom brought to the job an enduring
commitment to developmentally handicapped children.

A letter from the mother of a former Ives student, dated
August 26, 1967, suggests the effect of the Ives program: "[A]ll
the children (Frank's brothers and sisters) are looking forward

to school starting, especially Frank, thanks to his former experiences under your tender care. We thank you again for all your time and loving concern for Frank. Good luck to you this year. May it be less hair-raising than last!"

NOTES

1. L.B. Ames, *Arnold Gesell, Themes of His Work* (New York: Human Sciences Press, 1989).
2. W.M. Cruickshank, F.A. Bentzen, F.H. Ratzenburg, and M.T. Tannhauser, *Teaching Method for Brain-Injured and Hyperactive Children: A Demonstration Pilot Study* (Syracuse, N.Y.: Syracuse University Press, 1961).
3. T.B. Weston, ed., *Some Approaches to Teaching Autistic Children* (London: Pergamon Press, 1965), xxi.
4. S. Elgar, "Teaching Autistic Children," in J.K. Wing, ed., *Early Childhood Autism* (London: Pergamon Press, 1966), 224–25.
5. N.C. Kephart, *The Slow Learner in the Classroom* (Columbus, Ohio: Charles E. Merrill Publishing House, 1960).
6. R.H. Barsch, *Achieving Perceptual-Motor Efficiency: A Space Oriented Approach to Learning*, vol. I of *A Perceptual Motor Curriculum* (Seattle: Special Child Publications, 1967). This book formed the basis for several courses at colleges for teachers at the time.
7. Cruickshank et al., op cit.

III • CASE STUDIES IN AUTISM: CHILDREN AND PARENTS

These are the stories of nine children who attended the Elizabeth Ives School for Special Children: Tom Brown, Polly Daniels, Jimmy Davis, Bill Kolinski, David Ellis, Karen Stanley, John Stark, Larry Perelli, and Eric Thomas. As children, all were diagnosed as "out of touch," "impervious," "unaware of the environment," with "inappropriate reactions to the environment," and, to a greater or lesser degree, all nine illustrate the traits which define autism: the concreteness of thought; inability to reason logically; speech, whether articulate but odd (John, Polly), limited and echolalic (Tom, Karen), or totally lacking (Eric, Jimmy); eyes that refuse to look directly at you (all nine children); stiff posture or ways of moving (David, Tom, Karen); compulsive gestures (Eric, Jimmy, Karen); fascination with repetitive movement (Karen, John, Tom); overwhelming anxiety communicated through posture, hair-triggered tantrums, the need for sameness and structure (all nine). At the same time, these nine demonstrate the great differences that exist among autistic individuals.

In the stories that follow, it should be kept in mind that there is a difficulty in the exact classification and diagnosis of each child; the behavioral abnormalities found in the spectrum of autistic disorders should not be regarded as rigid. Children can move from one group to another as they grow. Some, like Polly, may have autistic "overlays" behaviorally, but on the Autism Behavior Checklist score "probably not autistic."

Each case study describes the child's education, from diagnosis to the present day, and describes their various types of schooling, vocational workshops, and living situations.

At the end of seven of the case studies are the results of developmental testing performed in October 1987, when each was an adult and several years after each had finished his or her education. (Of the remaining two, one was unavailable for testing and the other had died.) The tests used were the Wechsler Adult Intelligence Scale-Revised (WAIS-R), the Vineland Adaptive Behavior Scales, and the Autism Behavior Checklist (ABC). Many factors—such as motivation, curiosity, creative talent, work habits, and achievement in particular academic subjects—are not measured by these or any other (intelligence) test, and that fact should be taken into account when interpreting these results.

The WAIS-R measures intellectual functioning. It has six subtests of language and verbal skills (the verbal IQ scale), and five subtests of perceptual motor or nonverbal solving ability (the performance IQ scale). Intelligence test scores reflect a sample of learning in several different skill areas, including factual knowledge, learned abilities, problem solving, memory, and attention. Therefore, these scores are generally good predictors of future learning, academic success, and other abilities although intelligence in any autistic individual is blurred by the effect of the disability, which does affect cognitive functioning.[1]

There is a lack of integration in the senses that affects the input from the apparently normal eyes and ears of autistics. Messages received by their brains do not convey a clear, understandable picture of what is seen and heard. The result of this deprivation is dramatic. If it is gross and prolonged, individuals may function as severely retarded. If they are of potentially normal cognitive development, recovery tends to be rapid once the environment is improved.[2]

The Vineland Adaptive Behavior Scales is a standardized instrument that, using interviews with a parent or primary caregiver, assesses a child's capacities for personal and social sufficiency in various areas (or domains) of functioning. These cover communication, daily living skills, socialization, and motor skills.

The Autism Behavior Checklist (ABC) represents an attempt made a dozen years ago to provide a diagnostic instrument for autism. It contains fifty-three items relevant for the diagnosis of pervasive developmental disorders. These items elicit clinical information, in this case from teachers, from which it is possible to provide a score that corresponds to symptom severity. The validity of the ABC has been extensively studied at the Yale Child Study Center by Dr. Fred Volkmar and colleagues. The weighted scores on the ABC can be used operationally to distinguish autistic from non-autistic individuals, although a clinical evaluation is necessary before a firm diagnosis of autism can be reached. Individuals with an ABC score of 67 or higher have a high probability of being autistic; those with scores in the 53 to 67 range are possibly autistic; and those with scores lower than 53 are unlikely to be autistic.[3]

The October 1987 testing was performed at the Yale Child Study Center under the supervision of Dr. Sara S. Sparrow, associate professor of psychology at the Yale Medical School and chief psychologist at the Yale Child Study Center. The testing itself was done by Alice Carter, Ph.D., assistant professor of psychology, and Fred Volkmar, M.D., director of the Sally Provence-Irving B. Harris Child Development Unit and assistant professor of psychiatry and pediatrics at the Yale Medical School. The ABC was rated in September 1987 by

Virginia W. Sperry, retired director of the Ives School, on all seven of the children as they were at ages four to eight.

Immediately following six of the case studies presented here are the stories of the parents. These were taken from taped interviews and written accounts and try to convey what it was like for each parent to discover that their child was autistic; what they did when they found out; and how they are coping today. As each child is different, so are the parents, although the general characteristics of autism provide a basis for similarities. For most parents, talking about themselves and their children was difficult—not because they didn't have a lot to say, but because it was hard for them to expose and re-experience the painful emotions that have gone with each stage of their child's life.

Many of these people are still angry and embittered. A few are resigned. One, Mrs. Davis, is thankful for her child as he is. And some live day to day, still fearing that their child may yet close up and become unreachable or, to use one mother's words, "back off the edge of the Earth and never return."

NOTES

1. L. Wing and A. Attwood, "Syndromes of Autism and Atypical Development," in D.J. Cohen and A.M. Donnellan, eds., *Handbook of Autism and Pervasive Developmental Disorders* (New York: John Wiley & Sons, 1987), 4.
2. Ibid.
3. F.R. Volkmar, D. Cicchetti, E. Dykens, S. Sparrow, J.F. Leckman, and D.J. Cohen, "An Evaluation of the Autistic Behavior Checklist," *Journal of Autism and Developmental Disorders* 18 (1)(1988): 83.

1 • ESSENTIALLY ISOLATED: TOM BROWN
born February 4, 1960

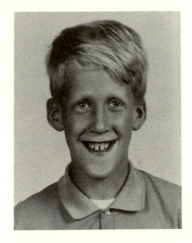

W hen Tom came to Ives, he was five years old and only whispered in two- or three-word sentences. He had been diagnosed at the Yale Child Study Center as having slow general development and an atypical (autistic) personality disorder. The physician who examined him at Yale noted that Tom had been an irritable, difficult-to-comfort infant who cried a great deal and could only be quieted by being rocked. He had no words until age two and was slow in motor development as well. On the developmental evaluation, he showed mildly uncoordinated motor functions but did well with structured materials, showing relatively good form perception. He could discriminate size and follow a pattern. Number concepts and motor control were his weakest areas. Language was a year below age, at a four-year-old level, and reasoning ability was at a three-year-old level. He appeared to have a neurological handicap that affected his body image and general perception of the world around him.

Tom's parents were described as sensitive people, and their concern had perhaps exaggerated his dependence. His clinging but oddly impersonal relationship with his mother was noteworthy. He was unusually sensitive to temperatures, sounds, and smells. He was especially vulnerable to anxiety and had difficulty in forming close relationships with others. He had problems in logical thinking and in differentiating reality from fantasy. He was considered more handicapped by the personality disorder than by his mild mental retardation. His parents were advised that he needed special education to address his social and emotional problems, as well as his difficulties in cognitive development. Shortly after undergoing this evaluation, Tom was referred to Ives, and he entered in the following fall.

Tom attended the Ives School for three years. In his first two months, he was quite passive and seemed content to follow his teacher's suggestions. He showed considerable diligence in the pursuit of his activities, often to the point of *perseveration*, and frequently, regardless of the task, he would stay at something until the teacher moved him to something new. Yet he displayed a lack of feeling about the results, showing neither pride nor pleasure nor anger. His conversation was limited to "What?," "No," and "Yes," and he was passive in the face of the aggressive acts of other children.

In the spring of his first year at Ives, Tom began to show signs of gradual gains. He became more negative to teachers' guidance and said "No" to any and all activities. The teachers were encouraged and felt that this "No" was at least the beginning of something other than an absence of recognizable reaction. Tom also made other kinds of progress. He now would move his chair away from an aggressor and react when displeased by spitting.

During this year, Tom used the most words while he was involved in doll or water play—to the doll, "You're a bad girl," or, to himself while washing doll dishes, "This is wet," or "That's a mess." His direct conversation with teachers consisted of "No" or naming objects in pictures. Otherwise he did not use words. At snack time, he pointed to what he wanted, and although he enjoyed the game of Lotto, he would reach for a card without saying the appropriate words. Although he would listen intently to stories read aloud, his facial expression remained dull, and unlike the other children, he never commented on the stories.

Tom had good form perception and was good with fairly difficult puzzles. But he seemed to have some visual-motor problems: He found it nearly impossible to stand one block on another in order, or to follow a block model. Nor could he think logically very well. Though he recognized color, he could not use it as a clue to proper placement of the blocks, and he could match colors but could not use them to follow a block pattern. In painting and drawing, he would color circles or primitive stick figures and immediately cover the picture with black.

By the end of his third year, Tom, at eight, was ready to go back to special education classes in public school. He was then reading in a preprimer. He was very distractible and still made compulsive flailing motions with his hands, but he played with other children, one at a time, and could talk audibly. He still had to be taught on a one-to-one basis.

Tom was seriously hampered by his bland *affect*. People tended to treat him as a cipher. But the conclusion of the teachers at Ives (which has been shared by many since who have come to know Tom) was that Tom knew more and felt more than he was able to express.

An Ives School teacher's report dated in the spring of Tom's departure gives this picture of him:

> Tom still does not really interact with other children. Although there is considerably more direct contact between Tom and other children and also more direct conversation, nevertheless most of the time the contact remains indirect and experimental. In playing house for instance, he plays with the *teacher*. Outdoors, he is much more likely to appear to be playing with a child as they ride on bikes together. Indoors, the times that he has played with

classmates, involving reciprocal conversation, have been rare and usually have revolved around trucks and blocks. Tom is an imitator, picking up other children's provocative ways. He makes lots of noise with the sticks of the Lincoln logs (banging them on the table) or raising up the radiator cover and letting it fall with a bang, or (slyly) moving the large airplane close to the radiator and turning the propeller against the radiator. He has never hit or struck out at another child. He will flail at the air with his hands or he'll sometimes touch a child saying, "Stop that" or "That's not nice" or "Shut up!" He will sometimes footnote this in an aside to the teacher, saying "Hey, Jimmy's hitting me." His calling out of toilet words is much less frequent this year. When Tom does get really physically hurt, he gets very upset, reddening and tensing up, with tears in his eyes, looking hurt, resentful, and frustrated. He hardly ever verbalizes his feelings. If you do this for him, such as "That really hurt you, Tom, and it makes you very mad, doesn't it?," he sometimes acknowledges this with a lessening of the tension, a direct look in your eyes and a little half smile. When Tom makes a direct protest, it is done timidly and in a bland voice.

Physically and emotionally, Tom is hard for an adult to get close to. Many people in first dealing with him tend almost to forget his presence in the room. After long acquaintance, at least two of his teachers feel real affection, warmth, and understanding for him. Tom in this area, too, is making slowly improving attempts at direct personal contact. One day he concentrated on one teacher with abusive language and lots of loud nonsense talk. This was on the playground. She had to leave to go into the room and invited Tom to come help. He started to follow her in, but then would only yell at her, "Shut up, shut up." Just as she was getting to the door, she heard him say sweetly, "I'll be waiting for you." Also she was out on Monday. On Tuesday, Tom said softly to her, "We missed you yesterday."

Mrs. Brown's and Tom's goodbyes to each other are usually shy, with Tom normally turning his back but always taking a peek at her as she leaves. He runs to her gladly at the end of the school hours; however, there is never direct warmth. On her part, Mrs. Brown's caring for Tom, though undemonstrative, appears so deep and is so disturbing to her that one wonders how much of her anxiety Tom feels.

It is next to impossible for Tom to stay on a walking board or a balance board. In joining in a circle game, his gait is shambling and awkward. He does not skip yet and has trouble hopping. He is now working with another child in reading and enjoys the competition. He has a funny streak of stubbornness and on some days refuses to say vocabulary words aloud which he knows and you know he knows. This would tie in with the kind of uncooperative behavior he demonstrated toward the speech therapist at the Rehab Center. He many times refused to say things and told his mother later, "I didn't talk."

The report also discussed a difficult aspect of his personality:

Anyone who deals with Tom should be on the alert for his desire for special consideration and his hostility if this is not forthcoming. This quality may not be immediately apparent, but runs deep. It means he has keen feelings about one person relating consistently with him. In a teaching situation, this seems to be of primary importance.

On the subject of his stubbornness and quiet hostility, his mother, many years later, wrote: "I always felt that Tom's hesitancy to answer was his way of getting back. No one could make him talk. He always needed to be first."

Tom spent two years in the special education class in his public school system. At that point his family moved and he transferred to another school system where he again was in elementary special education classes. After elementary school, he moved on to the special education vocational high school.

According to his parents, Tom received excellent treatment there. The teachers were professional in their approach to the teaching of special children. Tom learned many life skills, such as how to use a savings account and how to bank his salary. Tom learned how to cook and read simple recipes, how to shop for groceries and add up the bill, and how to handle a telephone. He also learned to read simple maps.

During high school, he was *mainstreamed* for sports, music, and art. Although he was still quite inarticulate, he nevertheless handled himself well with "normal" children and was well liked by the teenagers in his regular class.

During summers and during afternoons in the winter, Tom went to Saltaire, a Department of Mental Retardation regional center, for practical job training in work skills and for specific vocational courses such as dishwashing. On weekends he worked as a dishwasher in a small local restaurant.

Tom seems to have considerable ability. Although throughout high school he continued to have trouble speaking directly and audibly and had difficulty with logical thinking, he always gave other people, including his teachers, the impression that he had more ability than he was able to demonstrate. His Saltaire guidance counselor also said, "He can do more than just wash dishes."

At age twenty, Tom graduated from his vocational training class in high school. After graduation, he worked in a job as a dishwasher from noon to 5 P.M. each afternoon for the same restaurant where he had worked before. His employer was very pleased with the way he worked; in one of her reports, she said, "We do not have enough business to use Tom for longer hours. But he clearly hates to leave the restaurant so deliberately slows down on his dishwashing!"

As an adult, Tom has proven to be quite independent. He holds down a job and travels to it on his bicycle. He banks all of his salary and, by the age of twenty, had saved $2,000. He can make out deposit and withdrawal slips with help from his parents. He buys his own clothes, magazines, and records. Through the Saltaire Regional Center, he has become involved in several recreational events. He bowls every Saturday and is good at it; he has his own bowling ball. He goes square dancing with a group sponsored by the Association for Retarded Adults and is a skillful dancer. There are frequent summer picnics and winter parties. Tom's mother reported that though he speaks infrequently, he is liked by everyone, and at school he always had a friendly group around him. At Saltaire he developed socially. Tom enjoyed staying overnight at the camp, allowing his family to take short vacations.

Tom's independence has had its trouble spots. He startled his mother by twice leaving the house and disappearing for several hours. Each time he went on his bike to Saltaire to see his friends, and from there went straight to work, on time. But he did not understand that he needed to communicate this fact to his mother.

Most of the time, however, Tom is at home. There, he spends a lot of time in his room listening to records, and he used to spend hours playing with computer games. He has a tape recorder and talks into it a great deal. His mother has never listened to the tapes. He watches a lot of television.

One of Tom's main problems is lack of social initiative. A good example of his level of social interaction occurred one summer at a picnic. He took his parents to meet his friend, a forty-year-old retarded woman with whom he had been bowling. The introductions made, Tom ignored his parents and stood beside his friend most of the evening, neither one of them talking.

His interaction with his family remains more a matter of

everyday routine. He talks very little and, unless forced, avoids all eye contact. This has been quite difficult for his parents over time. His mother once said bitterly that retarded children were supposed to be rewarding and affectionate, but neither she nor her husband has ever felt that Tom is fond of them. Mrs. Brown is a tall, gentle person, who, though she cried easily when Tom was young, has resilience, strength, and a sense of humor. Intelligent and decisive, she had difficulty with Tom's disability when he was young, but gradually acquired self-confidence in dealing with the issues involved. Both parents are well-educated, professional people.

Socially, things have been often difficult for the family. If the parents go to a party where Tom can "fit," they take him. He tends to spend such evenings sitting, smiling occasionally, talking to no one except when spoken to, apparently content in his isolation. Mrs. Brown finds introducing him gracefully an insoluble problem. As she said, "I can't say 'This is Tom, my retarded son.' " Both parents are keenly aware that people meeting Tom are thinking, "What is wrong with him?"

Tom's parents know that Tom, being as independent as he is, needs some basic sex education. Tom's mother once attended a lecture on sex education for the mentally retarded, and enrolled him in a twenty-three-week Planned Parenthood class on sex education. While he is not sexually active, Tom is aware of sex; he spends a lot of time in the bathroom, "masturbating probably," according to his mother.

The final and biggest question has become, of course, what to do about an adult Tom. His degree of independence poses some critical questions. How could he have sensible independence and yet still be looked after? At the age of twenty-one, a legal guardian needed to be appointed for him, but this was only done ten years later. Where should his parents go for the proper legal advice?

Tom's parents have always been concerned about Tom's

aloneness. One solution they seriously considered was to buy a condominium for him and his sister, who is also developmentally handicapped, but less so than Tom. After some consideration, Mr. and Mrs. Brown decided not to put the responsibility for Tom onto his sister's shoulders. They realize that he should be living in a group home or some supervised apartment-type living arrangement, but deinstitutionalization of the handicapped has placed formerly institutionalized people in alternative living arrangements ahead of those who already live in good homes. And so new living opportunities for Tom have not opened up.

Plans to place Tom in a group home were discarded when he had a seizure at the age of twenty-eight. He was at home in the kitchen when it hit him, causing him to fall, unconscious and face downward, into a sink full of dirty dishes, his long arms extending over the counters on either side. Both parents came running and carefully picked him up and stretched him out on the floor. Tom came to within five minutes but remembered nothing. He went back to work and seemed fully recovered. A complete neurological exam disclosed no abnormality that would explain the seizure, and there has never been a recurrence.

The Browns are still determined, however, to find an answer that would ameliorate Tom's isolation and allow him more companionship with peers.

Tom now works a full day as a dishwasher. His boss and his coworkers all view him with affectionate understanding and are supportive yet firm. The seizure does not seem to have affected his work at all. He is able to function independently, with all the people in the restaurant around, without getting flustered or withdrawn. For example, he can now select his own lunch from the multitude of choices. Until recently, he had required help with this.

Tom now rides his bike not only to work, but to the barber

and to several stores where he buys tapes, magazines, and clothes. At the bank, he now makes out his own withdrawal and deposit slips. By the time he was thirty, he had over $15,000 of his salary saved.

In spite of his essential isolation, Tom has a busy social life. Although he has developed comparative autonomy, he still follows the pattern of his late teenage years. He does chores at home and cooks for himself. He has no peer companionship, other than those he sees during any of his structured social activities, such as bowling and square dancing. He does not go to friends' houses, nor do any friends come to his.

Tom's sister works at a big supermarket and can carry on a conversation with some give-and-take, which is almost impossible for Tom. She has two good friends, with whom she goes to movies and to programs at the nearby Center for the Developmentally Disabled. The dilemma for Tom's parents is that, although it is a temptation to ask his sister to include him on her outings, they feel it would be unfair to do so.

Though it is lonely, Tom's life is fairly contented. In the summer, his family vacations at a lake, where Tom swims and fishes. His family goes out to dinner frequently both at home and on vacations, and this contributes to Tom's social experience. Nevertheless, despite Tom's apparent stability in his job and other routines, his family, especially his mother, continues to experience the strain and frequent distress that comes with having to care for an adult with special needs.

As an adult, Tom Brown stands six feet two inches tall. He is blonde and blue-eyed and often smiles shyly. His shoulders are broad, his whole body strong and healthy. He no longer resembles the thin, gangly, somewhat awkward, bland-looking child and teenager he once was. Yet today he still cannot look anyone straight in the eye: He glances to one side or the other. His voice is soft and the sentences abbreviated, sometimes deteriorating into an unintelligible mutter. It is in this that he most vividly recalls the five-year-old boy who first came to Ives.

When Tom was thirteen years and seven months old, he was given a psychological evaluation by his local school system at the request of his parents. On the Wechsler Intelligence Scale for Children, he scored an IQ of 55. He failed every item on the Bender Visual Motor Gestalt Test.

In June 1981, at the age of twenty-one, Tom received psychological and vocational testing. He was neatly and appropriately dressed. His behavior during testing was exemplary. The psychologist, who considered the test a valid measure of Tom's ability, reports:

> Tom presented himself for testing as a quiet but friendly twenty-one-year-old young man. During testing, he exhibited a sustained level of concentration and attention throughout. He approached each task with an air of confidence.
>
> Tom's current level of intellectual functioning falls in the upper limits of the Mentally Deficient range. There is no significant difference between verbal and performance abilities.
>
> In the verbal areas, Tom's strength is his ability in abstract reasoning or logical thinking, which is average. His word knowledge is borderline, while abilities in general, judgment and common sense, arithmetic skills, and short-term memory for numbers are very deficient. . . .
>
> On the Bender Gestalt, a measure of visual motor coordination, Tom's performance is indicative of an individual having serious visual motor difficulties which suggest organicity. . . .
>
> Tom's academic achievement as measured by the Peabody Individual Achievement Test is at a grade three level for overall achievement. His ability in mathematics, which

is his lowest academic area, is limited to counting items
from one to twenty; simple addition and subtraction of
whole numbers up to six; number recognition at least to
thirty; and knowledge of the idea of what an object that
has been cut in half looks like. In word recognition, Tom's
highest academic area, Tom's ability is at a mid-grade four
level. Reading Comprehension is at a grade three level. . . .
Tom's fund of general knowledge is equal to individuals
functioning at a high grade three level.

The report then discusses the results of Tom's vocational
testing:

Individuals with abilities in this range (upper extended
level of competency) such as Tom, have the verbal-cogni-
tive ability to understand simple concepts and analogies
and can superficially relate these to their environment.
These individuals often do not internalize concepts and
therefore have difficulty generalizing from one set of circumstances to another.

The report goes on to say that although Tom shows
mild motor deficits that would ordinarily indicate a sheltered
workshop environment, he had proved that he could work
successfully in the community. His motor abilities "are sufficiently developed to allow for safe operation of some air-
powered and motor-driven equipment under close supervision.
Tasks requiring a fifteen- to thirty-minute time period for
completion can be performed by Tom."

In summarizing his impressions of Tom and the test results,
the psychologist depicts Tom as a pleasant young man who
appears shy but confident of his abilities. He describes him as
being unable to initiate conversation and incapable of understanding or relating to the emotional needs of others. He has
difficulty in gaining meaning from his experiences and has a

shallow contact with the environment. During testing, Tom
made little if any eye contact with the examiner.

The report concludes:

> Although [Tom] seems content with himself, he ex-
> presses the desire to be smarter. There seems to be some
> insight, although limited, into the fact that his abilities are
> limited. On the surface, these feelings of inadequacy are
> not readily apparent. There is an internal disappointment
> in the gap between aspiration and the ability to achieve.
>
> Tom appears to have some behavioral strengths. Pa-
> tience, high frustration tolerance, persistence in performing
> work tasks, good concentration, a cooperative nature and
> pleasant personality. . . .
>
> Behaviorally, Tom has many emotional and coping skills
> which he utilizes to his benefit. His limitations in this area
> are socialization and his inability to understand the impact
> of his behavior on others. . . . Tom seems to be able
> to perform at a slightly higher level than test results
> indicate. . . .

Tom was twenty-seven in October 1987, when he was
tested at the Yale Child Study Center. Tom's scores were
as follows:

WAIS-R

Verbal IQ: 64	Performance IQ: 69	Full Scale IQ: 65

VINELAND

Domain	Standard Score	Adaptive Level	Age Equivalent
Communication:	38	Weak	7 yrs. 11 mos.
Daily Living:	80	Moderate-low	13 yrs. 9 mos.
Socialization:	83	Moderate-low	15 yrs. 6 mos.
Adaptive Behavior Composite:	62	Low	12 yrs. 5 mos.

ABC
107: Quite autistic

There is no doubt that Tom constitutes something of a triumph
over the disabilities of autism in that he has achieved comparative independence. He is engaged enough in reality to take pride
in doing a job well, and he has a well-developed sense of
responsibility. He is, of course, still characterized by the basic
traits of autism, but he has developed far from the almost
nonverbal little boy who first came to Ives.

"It takes endurance
to stand up for your child . . ."

by Pat Brown

Tom was just over a year old when we moved to Connecticut. I was then pregnant, expecting our daughter Jennifer, and moving was a trauma. We moved in February and maybe it was the new situation, but Tom just seemed to feel very uncomfortable. He cried all the time. I felt that something was wrong with him. He didn't appear to be developing properly, and he was so easily upset by people. He just cried and cried, which was very frustrating. Our pediatrician reassured me that Tom did not have anything wrong with him, that he was a middle child, and that his being a middle child might explain his being socially upset.

Tom didn't like to be with other people. I can remember sitting outside with other women and children. He would climb onto me to be away from them, but he couldn't settle down even then and kept fidgeting. He didn't walk until late, and he didn't want to feed himself. He was very interested in things that spun and in any toys that moved. He would watch the wind in the trees, waving his arms and flapping his hands. He used to flap his hands when the automatic garage door closed. (As an adult, he still likes to watch the garage door close.)

I think Tom must have been two when the pediatrician finally sent me to the Yale Child Study Center. There they didn't give any specific diagnosis; they just said he was atypical with autistic tendencies. All they gave me was oral information, nothing in writing. That was their policy at the time. They would write letters to school, but they would not give a parent a written diagnosis. I never got a written diagnosis until Tom was twenty-one.

I don't know when we learned he was autistic. It was probably when he was about four, I went to register him for nursery school. The people at the school said that he was not the sort of child they could take. We had him tested [at the Yale Child Study Center], and the results showed that he was mildly retarded. They said he had "autistic tendencies" and was "mildly retarded," but they never said that he was an autistic child. They never had a definite reason for Tom's problems. We never knew until just within the past year what caused it.

Finally, last year, Tom was diagnosed as *Fragile X positive*. It's helpful finally to have a definite diagnosis. My husband, Steve, definitely found it a help, and it's now very plain that Tom's sister, Jennifer, has the same thing. Evidently, it's a genetic abnormality on my side of the family, which bothered me, but I can't think of anyone in my family, except perhaps one uncle, who might also have had it. They said sometimes several generations pass without it showing up. They also told me that one of the signs of being a carrier is crying all the time for no reason. I do that.

Tom attended Ives, and after Ives he went to public school, which worked out very well. Tom's special education teachers did a lot for Tom, and I was very pleased with what they did. I also admired their patience. The only difficulty I had with the public schools occurred when we moved, a few years after Tom started the special education program. I spoke to the head of special education at the public school in the town we were moving to and arranged for Tom's schooling there. I told her about Tom and gave her all his records, but when September came, they hadn't done anything. They weren't sure where they were going to place him at all. They thought they might put him in the same class as his sister. I got quite upset, since I had always tried to keep the two apart in school. The school system ended up putting Tom in a junior high special education program at the last minute.

Ultimately, the public school special education programs were very good for Tom. He got a lot of help, and his teachers worked with the State Department of Mental Retardation to get him job training after he left high school. He trained at the local regional center to learn dishwashing.

We had more difficulty from the public schools with Jennifer. When she was going into first grade, after having failed kindergarten, her psychologist at the Yale Child Study Center recommended that she go to a certain special school, which had a good learning-disabled program. Everything was arranged when the public school system, which is responsible for paying the tuition for such special schools, up and decided that because the Yale Child Study Center had merely suggested that this would be good for her, not insisted on it, the school system was not going to pay the $1,200-per-year tuition. Eight years later, we finally sent Jennifer to a private residential school that cost $13,000 a year, which, of course, the public school system ended up having to pay for anyway.

In dealing with all of the administrative issues that come up when you have a special child, it's very difficult if you don't have a lawyer working for you. Money is always the issue, and although I think things have improved because now there are more laws requiring that public school money be spent on special children, it still takes a lot of endurance and gumption to stand up and fight for your child. For me it did.

Since 1979, when he left high school, Tom has had the same job, which he got through the regional training center. He washes dishes and does some cleaning. He has picked up some other skills, such as peeling and washing potatoes. He goes to his job five days a week, and he's always there ahead of time, after a four-mile ride on his bicycle.

Jennifer has an apartment with a roommate, but Tom still lives at home. He doesn't relate much to us. He talks to his sister on the phone and they seem to have wonderful conversations. I don't know why, but he talks to other people much more than he talks to us. I think somehow we inhibit him. We've always controlled him, and he has the need to be in charge of the situation.

He performs his jobs around the house promptly without being reminded—things like emptying the trash and the dishwasher, helping to cook. He seems to enjoy basic cooking and will probably learn more. He knows how to use the dishwasher, washing machine, dryer, stove, and microwave, although he usually needs help deciphering directions for the microwave.

He uses the telephone well. He remembers numbers: social security number, bank account, telephone numbers. He goes to the bank by himself to deposit his check and make withdrawals, but he needs help balancing his checkbook. He loves to buy things, but he never asks to buy anything or wants to buy anything on his own. For the last ten years he's had the same things on his Christmas list. He goes to the barber shop by himself when he is reminded. He seems to read the newspapers but never comments on what he reads.

Tom has always been interested in plants and keeps track of the temperature and barometric pressure in the house. Once I was concerned about his losing weight, so now he weighs himself every week and writes it on the chart. He has a cassette recorder and listens to the same tapes over and over again. When he's watching television, if people come up and say hello, he doesn't say hello out loud. He just sits there and bows.

He enjoys social activities with people his own age, but he has no close friends and doesn't make any contacts on his own. He likes sports and has become a very good bowler. He has also become very good at playing a number of computer games. These involve a good deal of manual dexterity, and he has a good memory for them.

He does require help with money arrangements of any kind, with hygiene, such as when to shave, and, at times, with appropriate dress. He doesn't know how to use public transportation either, but I think he could probably learn.

He is somewhat of a mystery, and I think he is capable of doing much more than he does, particularly with things that do not require judgment and logic. Tom can learn to do many things perfectly. He runs machines really well. His only difficulty comes if something goes wrong. He isn't able to ask for help. Once he broke the aquarium in his room and tried to soak up the water with bath towels. We found out about it when we noticed that the downstairs ceiling was damp. He couldn't explain why he hadn't told us about it, but that is his normal way of dealing with problems. You have to be sensitive to the nonverbal clues to find out that something is wrong, since he will never volunteer the information, even though he needs your help to fix the problem.

Sometimes Tom just doesn't seem to deal with reality. One weekend we asked if he wanted to go to ceramics or golf. And he said ceramics. I said, "Do you know what ceramics is?" And he said, "No." And so I explained. "Oh yeah," he said. "That sounds really great." But when I mentioned taking golf lessons, he said, "Golf?" as if he didn't know what it was. And his father plays golf all the time.

You are never really sure if he quite understands. And sometimes when we're doing things you can see he's just confused. He doesn't know which way to turn sometimes. When we're walking down the street or going somewhere, he's sometimes not quite there. You can see this look in his eyes.

Tom has never yelled or shouted or gotten angry in a way I could tell by the sound of his voice. He will throw or break things when he's frustrated, though, and we explain to him that we know he's angry because he broke something. I think he doesn't know how to express his frustration in words.

I think that autistic people are very aware of everything, but they just don't or can't admit or express it. They can almost reach into your mind at times, as if they know what you are going to do next, even before you do. It's as if they pick up on a signal that you give out. I think Tom is this way. He seems to know everything I'm going to do, and he always will. If I'm going to get up out of a chair, he'll get up first. I talked to some other relatives of autistic people down at Yale, and they said similar things.

Recently we finally acquired a guardianship for Tom through the probate court. We asked for a full guardianship, but they said they very rarely give them because they like the handicapped person to be able make some decisions for him- or herself. So Tom and I went to a meeting with the Department of Mental Retardation. Unfortunately, I started crying, as usual, and I think that influenced the department's decision. I didn't really want the representative to change her mind because of that; I wanted to convince her of the merits of my position. As a compromise, she asked if Tom could be allowed to make decisions about his living situation. I said of course he could, but that at the moment we couldn't find anything available. They ended up recommending that we get full guardianship, and I felt a bit guilty because I thought I changed their mind by crying.

Recently we also got Tom into a Planned Parenthood class on sex education, which goes on for twenty-three weeks. He has gone twice. It's not only sex education but also how to behave in the community, proper hygiene, and such things. Someone from the Department of Mental Retardation is there to work with the Planned Parenthood people. I tried to ask Tom what they talked about in class. He finally said, "Where babies come from." I said, "Well, where do babies come from?" And he said, "I don't know." I had been concerned about Tom's sexual awareness because when we filled out a form about his bowling, he wrote something on a piece of paper and stuck it on the outside of the envelope. It said something about watching a woman teacher—the one the envelope was going to—walking around the street with no clothes on. The teacher called and told us about it. We talked to Tom about this incident and said that it's not appropriate. You can think these things, but you can't write them in letters.

Also, for years he has used the term "wa-wa." I don't know what that means. He had a note from a girl at work last summer, a waitress who'd written to him. She mentioned the word, and he wrote her a note I found that said he wanted to do the wa-wa with her. I asked people at his job and in his bowling group what it means. The lady at work said it's some kind of a dance. The woman who took Tom and his friends bowling said that the kids, whenever they were asked what kind of music they wanted to hear, would all say "wa-wa music." She didn't really know what it meant either. I've tried to tell Tom that it upsets me when he says "wa-wa" because I don't know what it means, but he can't tell me what it means. I don't know if he actually knows.

Tom should be in a group home, but I think that putting him in one would be very traumatic for him. It's also hard to find a job and a live-in situation that are close enough together. I've turned down a couple of options because they were too far away from his job. A group home would be much better for Tom because he sort of isolates himself at home. He's protected here, but he doesn't have much communication with my husband and me or with other people.

Tom's sister, Jennifer, lives in a condominium we bought for her. Since Tom has saved a good deal of money, it might be possible for him to buy into some kind of apartment or live-in situation. Tom's caseworker at the Department of Mental Retardation has been talking about apartments. But although Tom could very well take care of himself, an apartment, and cooking if someone came in each day, I would still be concerned about his isolation, even if he had a roommate. He takes no initiative with his social life. He loves to go out if someone else plans something, but he doesn't make any plans himself. I can see Tom sitting in his apartment, going to work, going dancing on Friday (because he does that every Friday), but not ever telling his roommate or neighbors what he does. Jennifer's roommate organizes all kinds of things, and that's great for Jennifer. What Tom really needs is some sort of warm atmosphere where he can be with a group of people. That would give him something to do, and people to relate to. We have had Tom's caseworker get him on the list for a group home.

There is one place I know near here where they have a number of apartments in one building and twenty-four-hour supervision. I'm thinking about trying to get Tom in there. There's always a long list for placement, but that's the kind of thing I'm thinking of. It's very similar to what we did with Jennifer. She's getting services through the Department of Mental Retardation, and in case something did happen with us—if we moved, for instance—she is settled. If we ever moved, we would not take Tom or Jennifer with us.

Another thing that has put Tom's living situation on hold is the proposed state budget cuts for the handicapped. Cuts are hitting the recreation programs too. The entire recreation staff in our district was laid off for a while. The Department of Mental Retardation recreation program has provided Tom with most of his outside activities. They have had a lot of their own programs and they ran all the Special Olympics programs, which they don't do in most of the state. The recreation people got their jobs back, but their transportation budget has been cut, so they aren't doing as much as they did. They have come up with a program on Thursday nights, which unfortunately is the night my husband and I go down to New Haven to attend a meeting for parents of adult autistics at the Connecticut Mental Health Center. The recreation staff used to have a party or other social event once a month, but they don't any more.

They had a party once this winter, but parents had to bring their kids themselves. They came up with the idea of taxi vouchers, which they sold for $1.60, so the kids could take a taxi. Jennifer and her roommate have used those a lot. Tom's never taken a taxi, so he didn't use the vouchers himself. We were going to the theater that night, so we drove Jennifer, her roommate, and Tom to the party. The girls took Tom to their condominium in the taxi after the party, and we picked him up from there when we got out of the theater.

We go with Tom to the autism clinic at the Connecticut Mental Health Center in New Haven, and I think it's good for him to go there. I feel at least there's someone I can go to if I need help. They're willing to deal with any sort of problem, and they can point us in the right direction. I've had a lot of help from the Department of Mental Retardation and our caseworker. I've learned to use them much more within the past three or four years. It's good to know there is someone who is aware of Tom, who knows that he's looking for a place to live and knows what my intentions are for Tom. I now feel I have some control over his situation.

The way the system works is this: The public schools legally provide funding and services, so they are in control. Once Tom was school age, he was involved in that. Today you'd be involved even early on through the early-intervention programs, but at the time Tom was young, it was just the school system. We went to Yale, had Tom diagnosed, and sent him to the Ives School without anyone really helping us. Only when Tom was enrolled in the public school system was there a single bureaucracy interested in his welfare and future.

The system works well until the kids get out of the school system when they are twenty-one. Then the parents are back almost on their own. You are supposed to go to the Department of Mental Retardation for help, but it's up to the parents to know all this. Every year the parents have to make arrangements and figure out what's going to happen in that year. And each year you find out that this program's stopping, or this person says your child should be going here, or that person says he should be going there. It seems like you go to one place and they deal with a certain problem, and then you go somewhere else and start all over again explaining the whole thing. There's no coordination. So you're supposed to deal with all of these different support systems. There's really no one single place you can go. No one is actually in charge except the parent.

It is frustrating to deal with all of the different agencies and doctors. It's just up to the parents, and it gets to be kind of a drag. I'm tired of thinking about Tom. Sometimes it seems that's all I do. Every time there's someone new; the professional people come and go. And then you're back to square one. A better system of coordinating the agencies must be developed.

2 • A PROFOUND COMMUNICATION DISORDER: JIMMY DAVIS
born September 22, 1962

At the age of three, because of a delay in his speech development, Jimmy Davis was referred to the Connecticut Department of Health's New Haven Evaluation and Counseling Program for Retarded Children. The physical and neurological examinations he received there did not reveal a cause for the delay: His hearing was normal, and he already wore glasses for nearsightedness. The testing did find, however, that his mental development was at the two-year-old level. The physician at the speech and hearing clinic said, "Jimmy closes people out." Subsequently, a public-health nurse who visited his home described him as "in a world of his own" but permitting brief periods of interpersonal contact.

Between the ages of three and four, Jimmy attended a small nursery school, but the experience was unsuccessful. The school's report on Jimmy stated:

> The only way in which Jimmy could be present at group activities was by the teacher holding him on her lap. This he liked. He enjoyed water play but had to be watched closely at it. One day he tried to push the tub which contained the water; he became frustrated because he could not move it and had a tantrum which frightened the other children. He jumped kicked, screamed, bit, and hit his head with his hands very hard.

During the time he attended this school, Jimmy was evaluated by several clinics at Yale-New Haven Hospital, and also by the local state-run rehabilitation center. Each evaluation gave a similar diagnosis: organic brain damage and retardation. His parents were a bit confused by this, as Jimmy appeared intelligent and was responsible for caring for himself at home. The pediatric specialist at Yale-New Haven's child development unit explained that though Jimmy in all probability had some brain impairment, he was, above all, disabled by his emotional disturbance, which left him afraid, angry, very upset, and puzzled. With no ability to talk out his problems, the physician said, Jimmy would behave as if he were retarded and would have the same needs as a such a child.

At four-and-a-half, Jimmy was diagnosed at the Yale Child Study Center as emotionally disturbed with conspicuous autistic symptoms. His maturational age was two years. He was described as a nice-looking, robust child who was clearly aware of others but who often avoided social contact. His speech remained markedly delayed and garbled (in fact, he has remained basically nonverbal all his life), and his parents were concerned about hyperactivity as well.

Jimmy's erratic response to formal testing made it impossible to assign a global development level. A series of individual sessions over several months at the Yale Child Study Center helped to clarify the disabling nature of his autistic personality. Jimmy responded positively to the individual sessions with a teacher, and on the basis of that he was referred to the Ives School that summer.

During Jimmy's first weeks at Ives, he behaved like a madman. He pinched, scratched, and screamed. He liked to butt people in the stomach, and he bit children and teachers. He was totally self-absorbed, keeping his head down and his eyes covered with one hand, successfully avoiding having to look at anyone. Outdoors, he sat in the sandpile and poured sand on his head or ate it. He walked around the play yard protected by the arm of a teacher, again shading his eyes, as though he was unbearably afraid of the world. During the fall and winter, on outings to the park, he insisted on walking buttoned up inside his teacher's coat, which created the rather strange apparition of a person with one head, a very fat stomach, two large feet, and two small ones.

By October, Jimmy was putting sand in containers and eating less of it. He had learned to use the slide, had climbed two rungs on the jungle gym, and used both the glider—a swing with two seats—and the single swings. Using the glider meant that Jimmy had to work with another child, an important step out of his self-imposed isolation. Indoors, he began putting together puzzles and snap beads, but he had no tolerance for failure. One mistake brought on a tantrum. He could be moody and withdrawn. Often, in those weeks, he worked in a room alone with one teacher. Because he still sometimes resorted to scratching, butting, and biting, one of the staff checked frequently to be sure that his teacher was surviving.

In June, at the end of that first year, Jimmy, then almost six, held up his head and looked at people. He smiled and laughed. On walks that spring, Jimmy ran ahead with the other children. He still did not talk, but he clearly understood what he was told, enjoyed listening to stories, and followed instructions if he happened to be in a cooperative mood.

While Jimmy improved in his first year at the preschool, he regressed the second year. He became increasingly belligerent and by February could tolerate being with only two children. He often had to go back to the one-room, one-teacher routine. The February report said, "Jimmy is a pathetic little boy, scared, insecure, with a poor self-image." As spring advanced, he resisted doing puzzles, coloring, and all the other nursery school activities he had enjoyed. Outdoors, he sat on the edge of the sandpile, his head buried in his teacher's lap. He appeared to have become overwhelmingly afraid again of the outside world and to feel safe only when protected by his self-isolation.

Gradually it became clear that it would be impossible to keep Jimmy at Ives. There were some difficulties at his home between his father and mother, and the teachers at Ives felt that this accounted for the change in his behavior. There was no other available school at the time, so the doctor at the Yale Child Study Center decided residential care was the best solution. Mrs. Davis consented, and she cooperated with the doctor in finding an appropriate setting.

The final report from Ives to the Yale Child Study Center and the public school system said, "Jimmy has the knack of finding his way into your affections. We are all devoted to him and have been fighting for him to the best of our abilities. He can be charming and appealing. He obviously has deep feelings blocked completely by his lack of ability to talk." The letter ended by saying, "We remain convinced that there is real potential here and all of us hate to 'give up' on him."

From Ives, Jimmy went to a regional residential school for the emotionally disturbed and the retarded located in a nearby town. This school had a wide spread in the age range of its residents, from preschoolers to forty-year-old adults. Jimmy stayed here for five years, but it was ultimately an unsuccessful experience. Some of his clothes were stolen, and he was overmedicated because of inadequate supervision. Consequently, his mother began to insist that he come back to live at home. She had divorced Jimmy's father, and guided by the Ives School social worker, she had been able to improve her home situation. She wanted to take total responsibility for Jimmy and felt she could create a more stable and supportive environment for him.

At that time, the Connecticut State Department of Education began funding a communication disorders program specifically for children with severe developmental disabilities. Jimmy transferred to this program when he was eleven, and because the public school in his hometown had started a facility under this program, he was able to return home to live. When Jimmy entered the communication disorders program, he was aggressive, phobic about animals, and hyperactive. After intensive work by his teachers, this behavior lessened, and he began to calm down as he developed a little self-confidence.

Jimmy's major accomplishment in these years was the improvement in his ability to communicate, achieved by teaching him to use sign language. At first, he used a combination of hearing aids in each ear and cassettes. The teacher showed him a picture, and a voice on the cassette said the name of the object pictured. The teacher made the appropriate sign, and Jimmy copied this signing. Once he possessed an adequate signing vocabulary, his intelligence was liberated, and his drive to achieve motivated and activated his learning. He made rapid progress and was soon moved to a higher-functioning group in the program. In the higher-functioning group, there were two teachers for a class of six children. Jimmy's potential was obvious to everyone from the beginning. He was aware of other people, and he became more responsive and continued to progress rapidly.

The program was well run, and parents received reports on the progress of their children and met monthly with the teachers. By the time Jimmy was seventeen, his mother had gone to business school and had remarried. Jimmy was then in his second year of high school. His mother and her new husband worked, she as a secretary at the hospital and he in business. Because of this, Jimmy was alone for forty-five minutes or so when he came home from school. He managed very well. He took the school bus, had his own key, and was quite self-sufficient. His ability to care for himself was considerable. He was particular about putting out his own clothes and being sure that they were matched. He cooked simple things such as eggs and hamburgers. He went to church every Sunday and was able to follow the service correctly. He could safely stay home alone if his parents went out in the evening. He enjoyed his stereo and television.

When Jimmy was twenty-one, he graduated from high school and entered a vocational training program. During the first year, he blossomed, learning, among other things, how to sort bolts and screws quickly and accurately. His instructor felt that Jimmy could be successful in a supervised vocational program or workshop, although his bent for teasing would make supervision tougher. Jimmy was expected eventually to be able to enter a group home, although his instructors felt that, for him to adapt well, the supervision would have to be very skilled and specialized, and the number of residents limited to four or five.

At twenty-five, Jimmy was given a formal communication evaluation to determine whether his communication could be improved. His workshop supervisor felt that a testing program at the local teachers' college might give a clearer diagnosis of Jimmy's basic problem. The clinician there described Jimmy as a pleasant young man, very cooperative, who concentrated for the entire hour-long testing session. He was responsive to short and simply phrased questions or statements but could not follow anything more complex. He exhibited his frustration at his inability to understand by loud vocal outbursts and waving or by persistent, protesting motions of his arms and hands. Stereotypic arm movements were occasionally noted, including frequent turning back and forth of his clenched left fist and looking at it with head bent and one eye as close as possible to his fist.

The evaluation concluded that Jimmy had a profound communication disorder secondary to mental retardation. The prognosis for any significant improvement in his verbal communication was poor, due to his neurological dysfunction. Nevertheless, the prognosis was good for further development of his communication skills through sign language. His excellent fine-motor skills, his ability to pay attention, his strong long-term memory, and his improved social interaction skills, plus a supportive family, made it likely that he would be successful in developing a good sign-language vocabulary. Unfortunately, at that time, because both his mother and his stepfather worked, there was no one to take Jimmy to the communication center at the teachers' college for lessons in sign language.

No WAIS-R, Vineland, or ABC scores are available. Jimmy's mother withdrew her permission for the testing in October 1987 because she felt the strange surroundings and change of routine would be too upsetting for him.

As an adult, Jimmy is a six-foot-tall, broad-shouldered man who stoops slightly. He dresses well and wears thick glasses and, often, a mischievous smile. He is only slightly verbal but is able to communicate with simple words, such as "food." He is able to express himself also through gestures and guttural sounds. He has shown great drive to succeed and to please, and in general he has done well. At the time of this report, Jimmy was considered the best worker in his shop and had been honored as "Worker of the Month" in the regional rehabilitation center's newspaper. He was on the waiting list for *supported employment*, most likely as a loader in a trucking company. He had been accepted in a group home but by his parents' request was continuing to live at home. There is no reason to doubt the soundness of their decision at this time.

"I thank God every day for Jimmy . . ."
by Victoria Davis

Jimmy is now twenty-nine, and he still works at the workshop. He has been doing pretty well; on one task they said he was the only one who could do it because he's so fast with his hands. He is a very good worker and has found favor with the people in the workshop. I just talked with Lisa, his social worker, whom I meet with once a year. She said he's doing well, no problem at all.

Once he had an outside job at the shipyard, but it didn't last. When he was working on the boats it was all right. He was good at the carpentry and things. But part of his job was to clean the bathrooms, and he didn't like that, although he did a good job. He began to behave inappropriately, especially with his laughter, so I said they should bring him back to the workshop. Maybe he was just not ready to get out there with so many people.

Now he goes to workshop Monday to Thursday. Jimmy gets up about 6 A.M., washes, and dresses himself. Then he goes downstairs and usually eats his breakfast before he goes to work. The bus picks him up at 8:15 or 8:30, and he gets back to the house about 3 P.M., except on Wednesday, when he gets home at 1 P.M.

He has a key and lets himself in. When he comes home, he puts his stuff away and then walks the dog. Usually he and my nephew walk the dog together, but if Jimmy is alone and has to walk the dog by himself, it is all right. He is able to cross the street by himself. After he finishes walking the dog, he lies down in bed and waits for me to come home from work. When it's time to cook dinner, he stays in the kitchen and, sometimes with my help, makes spaghetti or something simple. After dinner, usually either he watches television, or we sit around talking or popping popcorn. That's his daily routine.

Jimmy earns money at the workshop and is paid each week. The amount varies a lot, depending on his work. Sometimes he brings home $2, sometimes $3, sometimes $30 or $40. I think his biggest pay was when he was working at the shipyard, when he brought home about $78 a week. Of course, he uses his money and knows its value. He buys the paper, and he goes shopping and gets haircuts on Saturday. He reads the paper every day. He reads all the time. He gets four or five magazines a week. He has always loved books, too. When we go shopping he looks at the *Enquirer*, that dirt book with the movie stars, and the pornography.

Saturday is our shopping day. We always go shopping once a week. We used to go to Sears, but now we go to Caldor's or the mall. He likes to go to the amusement area in the basement of the mall and to the miniature sports car track outside. You should see him. Once he drove off the course, hit a tree, turned around, and kept going. He loves it.

On Sunday we go to church. We have our own church now, and I am the pastor. It's the Holiness Church of Jesus Christ Incorporated. We started it after my second husband, Jimmy's stepfather, passed away. He and I were going to do it together. It was something my husband dreamed of. After he passed, we got busy, and it was a challenge. Jimmy helps move the tables and carry the equipment, He sets up the instruments and takes up and blesses the altar.

Jimmy was very, very hurt when my husband passed. My husband had a heart attack, and Jimmy was there when he died. I was at work at the hospital. When I came home, I ran up the steps. Jimmy ran behind and saw how my husband was laid down in the bathroom. Later he kept trying to tell me to get my coat to go, because he thought my husband had been taken to the hospital. He kept looking and looking for him. He sat on the stairs and stayed there all night, so he knew something was different. Then the house was so full of people, and it was clear he knew something had happened. He kept looking out the window. That was sad. The people at church kept saying, "We're praying for Jim, because we know how attached he was to him." Now Jim understands when we go to the graveyard. He goes to the grave, and he says, "Daddy." I was very lucky to marry such a wonderful man the second time around. He was very good to Jimmy.

The only problem I have with Jimmy is sometimes he has restless nights. That's because he comes home from work and takes a nap. After that, he's up half the night. Sometimes, he's up until 3 A.M. watching television. When he goes to bed, he shuts the TV off, turns off the lights, and covers the birds—he has two birds, a cockatiel and a peach tree lovebird, which he feeds and takes care of.

One of the things that happened this year was television. Jimmy never used to pay any attention to television. We bought a new television for Christmas, and now he sits there with the remote control. You can't get it away from him. He hides it. He takes it when he goes to the bathroom. I don't even get a chance to watch it. So I watch television in my own room now.

He likes the Spanish station. He watches it so much I call him "Mr. Rodriguez," which makes him laugh. I notice that the Spanish station has a lot of festivities and Spanish girls dancing. He also likes the wildlife shows, with the different animals. He watches that off and on, and the programs where they're making things, like cabinets. He watches a variety of things.

Jimmy's at the age where he observes women. At church or wherever we go sometimes he is very aware of the opposite sex. He's fascinated by women's hair and by women with big busts, maybe because I'm heavy-busted. I think there are times he desires a woman because I think that part of him is normal and has that normal urge. Once he got into trouble because he masturbated on the bus. I think he still does it, but he does it at home discreetly. I've told him to go in his room and close his door if he has to because that's private, and he seems able to do that.

Jimmy sometimes acts up around women. Once he acted up so much on the bus that he got kicked off, and I think his getting overexcited about women was one of the things that caused that. But now, at home at least, he keeps his fooling under control. About two weeks ago he was fooling around before he went to work. So I talked with him, and my sister talked with him, and she stayed with him until he got on the bus to cool him down a bit.

Jimmy is a snappy dresser. He goes to Sears and picks out his own clothes. He has very good taste in clothes and likes expensive clothes. He has about seven or eight suits for going to church. I'm proud of him because he does look really very good when he's dressed up.

He still doesn't go to any social gatherings by himself. He spends time with my nephews, and his godmother takes him places, but most of the time he's with me. Since my husband died, he does not want to be too far away from me. It's been a year now, so we're hoping that will ease off and that I can go someplace myself occasionally.

When Jimmy was a little boy, he was shy and he kept his hands over his eyes all the time. Every now and then he still does that, but most of the time he observes. He is very much aware of what goes on, very aware of what's going on with the church, when we're supposed to be devotional, when we're supposed to take up the altar. He's very aware of everything in the house, too, and where everything is. If you want to know where something is, Jimmy will show you. Even when he and I get groceries, he knows what I get, what I buy. He's pretty much on top of things. I really thank God he's as well as he is.

I think things are pretty good for Jimmy. I don't have too many problems managing him. He's a big muscular man, but underneath all those muscles, he's really a pussycat. He loves me, respects me, and obeys me, and I don't have any trouble.

As long as I'm living, Jimmy will be living at home. As long as I'm in my right mind, as long as I'm able to, Jimmy will always be home. Home is very important to Jim. He has his own room. He has an apartment which I call "up in the attic," where he took a lot of his things, and where he spends a lot of time with his books.

He still has his dog. We call him "Mr. Bobo." Mr. Bobo has been with us since Jimmy was a little boy. We got him when Jimmy came back home from his residential school. He was afraid of dogs and was afraid to go outside, and so to help him we found a dog at the church boarding home. In the beginning, Jimmy used to get up on the table to get away from the dog, but after awhile he got to know Mr. Bobo, and now he loves him. And the dog loves him back. Jimmy takes him for walks, feeds him, and washes him. Mr. Bobo is a part of our life. He won Jimmy over, and now Jimmy is not afraid of dogs.

Jimmy has been a tremendous help to me in the house. He cleans, and he picks up anything that's out of place in the kitchen. When we're through with dinner he puts the dishes in the sink and cleans them up. He does not like his house to be messy. He takes the clothes downstairs to the washer for me. He vacuums. He rakes leaves in the yard. He's very good.

The only thing I find an obstacle in our life is that Jimmy still does not talk. If he could talk, I think it would be amazing what this boy could do.

I thank God for Jimmy. I really do. He has been a great help to me. He's always been there for me. When my husband died, he was still here for me, and we have a very beautiful relationship, mother and son. When he comes home from work, I always hug and kiss him and ask him how his day was. Before we leave we always hug one another, and I say, "Have a good day."

Jimmy has come a very, very long way. Somebody asked, "Who do you owe it to?" Well, I'll tell you. Being a religious person, being a minister, and being a servant of the most high God, I realize that my help comes from God, and I've realized through the years it was the Lord who brought me Jimmy. I thank God that I feel that I'm a good mother to Jim. There are times when I have lost patience, especially when he gets so overexcited, but through it all, I feel that I've been a good mother. And Jim has been a good son to me, as good as an autistic child can be. And I thank God because I find that he is much better. I've seen many autistic children and I think Jim has really come a long way. He does everything. I don't have to do anything for him but to take care of him and love him.

3 • A FRENETIC PERFECTIONIST: POLLY DANIELS

born October 16, 1959

As an infant, Polly was placid and lovely, a blessing to her mother, who already had active three- and four-year-old sons. But as time went on, her parents were troubled by her behavior. Polly was unusually passive and uncomplaining, watchful, and excessively quiet. She did not speak at all until she was two-and-a-half, and despite the optimism of Polly's doctors, her mother became increasingly disconcerted. When Polly was three-and-a-half, virtually overnight she began to talk in nonstop sentences. She also began to show extreme fear, often amounting to panic, in response to a variety of noises.

Between the ages of three-and-a-half and five, Polly increasingly displayed symptoms of a severe emotional disturbance: multiple irrational fears, temper tantrums, inability to play with others or to modulate and control her emotions. There were episodes during which she appeared quite psychotic. On top of this, when she was four, she had an extremely traumatic hospital experience related to a tonsillectomy.

At the age of four, Polly was treated at a local clinic and then later at the outpatient clinic of the Department of Mental Health, where she was diagnosed as *schizophrenic*. Shortly afterward, she was referred to the Yale Child Study Center, where an attempt at a more precise diagnosis was made. Polly's diagnosis was not clear, however, because along with a personality disturbance with autistic tendencies, she was found to have perceptual problems which only heightened confusion about her orientation to time, space, and reality. A treatment plan was developed at the Yale Child Study Center under which Polly would receive psychotherapy and attend a nursery school group at the center. There would also be social work counseling sessions for Mrs. Daniels to help her cope with the difficulties of living daily with Polly. It was hoped that this would not only help Polly and her family but would further clarify the diagnosis and identify what continuing kinds of services she might need.

Two years later, when Polly was six, she had made little improvement. She remained perplexing to all who knew her. At the nursery school she would scream, overturn furniture, and throw toys and juice cups. The teacher would try to help her regain control but had little success. Continued psychotherapy and placement in a therapeutic educational program were recommended. At seven, Polly was referred to the Ives School by her physician at the Yale Child Development Unit and her nursery school teacher.

The teacher's report from the nursery school said in part:

> Polly, originally referred to our clinic as a behavior problem, is a mixture of lovableness and exasperation to all who work with her. Her behavior ranges from angelic to impossible and even when she is being angelic one wonders when she will next explode, for her anxiety is tremendous and her impulse control extremely poor. She is plagued by various physical problems, particularly a skin condition which causes her to itch. A perceptual problem adds to Polly's emotional and physical difficulties, and this is an obvious interference in Polly's learning ability.

The report further described Polly as an appealing, attractive child who, although small, was physically strong. It also called her a "frenetic child." It concluded that "she is left-handed and is more skillful with the left side of her body." It recommended that a teacher "work with Polly on an individual basis," and that the teacher genuinely like Polly in order to help her like herself.

When she first arrived at Ives, Polly appeared a dainty, exquisitely dressed little lady. She was punctiliously obedient and eager to do everything her teacher suggested, almost before the fact—her anxiety was apparent in the tenseness of her movement, the excited speech mixed with stuttering, the often-repeated gestures of smoothing down her blonde hair—left hand, left side; right hand, right side.

But this was illusory: The petite charmer was a walking time bomb in a tense struggle to maintain control over herself. And if Polly was tense, so were her teachers, who waited apprehensively for the explosion. It finally came after four months at Ives. Polly remained controllable until the week before Christmas, when she began to slap people, throw things, yell, and kick. Neither her social worker at the Yale Child Study Center nor her teacher at Ives could explain what set it off. It might have been a visit to Santa Claus: Polly had been terrified of his beard and bushy hair. Whatever the cause, Polly could no longer maintain control and, under what must have been unbearable pressure, had fallen apart.

The difficulty was what to do about her outbursts. Physically, her teachers could not sustain two-and-a-half hours daily of volcanic behavior—hitting, kicking, throwing over the nursery-school table, biting, and screaming all the time. Even two teachers had trouble holding her.

Polly's psychiatrist, social worker, and teacher (with advice from the rest of the Ives staff) collectively arrived at a decision. They felt that Polly had been at Ives long enough to know that the teachers there cared about her. To the extent that she could feel safe, she felt safe with the people at Ives. They decided, in essence, to take a risk. They would try sending her home at the first hint of misbehavior and see if this produced a positive reaction. Polly's mother agreed, even though she had to make an hour-long round- trip between her home and the school, and there was now the possibility that Polly would remain in school for only fifteen minutes. Mrs. Daniels was willing to do it on the chance of helping Polly internalize some control.

The first day of this experiment, Polly's teachers told her repeatedly, "We care for you, but we don't like your behavior." That day she was sent home after she had been at school for only half-an-hour. Her mother reported that Polly, much upset at being sent home, covered up by pretending she had been at school the right amount of time. She was sent home three or four times at most. By the end of the week, her teachers knew, just by her demeanor when she entered the school, that she had made a decision. From that time on, she remained in control about three-quarters of the time, frequently responding to other children's teasing or provocation, "I will behave."

With Polly's improvement in behavior came improvements academically and in handling the equipment in the play yard. The teachers worked to increase her control and to reduce some of her anxiety. They worked particularly on her perceptual handicaps, specifically lack of depth perception. Her behavior at home also improved. By the time she was seven-and-a-half, after one school year at Ives, it was felt that Polly was ready to attend public school. After conferring with her teachers at Ives and her parents, the director of pupil personnel at the public school placed Polly in a learning disability class for younger children. She was to attend on a half-day basis.

By the time Polly left Ives, she had improved vastly. She could work a half-hour at a time at a table behind a screen (which was used to provide privacy in the classroom) in the company of up to three other children, as long as at least one teacher was there. She seemed to know most of her ABCs and had finished one story in a preprimer. She could "match" words (i.e., recognize that the word "dog" on a flash card was the same as the word "dog" on another flash card), and from this she had built a minimal vocabulary. Her retention of a word had to be as a whole word. Phonetics were impossible for her. Whether her problems stemmed from perceptual handicaps or the aggravated anxiety that accompanied them, or whether there was a problem with long term recall, was unclear at that time.

It was certain that Polly had severe perceptual handicaps, some in the area of depth perception. There were several clues to this: Polly could not master a balance toy known as "Bill Ding," which consisted of perhaps eight three-inch-tall wooden men, colored green or yellow, blue or red. The trick was to balance them one on top of the other, each standing on the shoulders of the one beneath. Polly could not place one man's feet squarely on the other's shoulders. She would turn the man sideways, so that his feet would be in the air, and he would fall, knocking over the first man. Polly showed extreme frustration at her failure to master this game. Her therapist also said that she could not make a coordinated design with colored shapes. He commented that it was extraordinary how poor her performance was when she was left to herself, and how difficult it was for her to learn from instruction.

Polly recognized that something was wrong with her, and her frustration increased. Her behavior in the play yard illustrated this. When she first came to Ives, she had frozen in terror on the bottom rung of the climber, but by the end of the year she could climb to the top. Nevertheless, when she attempted to lie flat on a slanted board used in balance training, which required her to lean over onto the inclined board, she was terrified. It was as if the board simply were not there. She would grasp the board with both hands, but her body would miss the board entirely, and she would fall flat on the ground. Then, aware of and disturbed by her failure, she would get up and run off to the swings.

Even at five, Polly could only manage stairs by crawling up each step, and she went through doorways as if she were blind, her hands outstretched to feel the emptiness.

Nevertheless, Polly had some real strengths. She had a good voice, and she sang on key and in rhythm. She loved music and dancing. Although she was a bit bossy with her peers, she had real leadership qualities. She was also determined to succeed, and put great energy into all her efforts at school. She was delighted with praise when she was successful, and correspondingly downcast and angered by her failures.

In September, when Polly went to public school for the first time, she spent one year in the class for the perceptually handicapped. During that year she was given a Stanford-Binet Intelligence Test and achieved an IQ score of 67. According to the test, at eight years, three months, she had a mental age of five years, nine months. Polly was consequently transferred to a class for the educable mentally retarded, where she remained until she graduated.

Polly made good progress at school, with only one major period of setbacks when she was twelve. At that time, Polly suffered two traumatic events. One was the departure of her grandparents for six months in Arizona for the first time. Polly was very close to them, and she projected her sense of loss by angry disruptive behavior and constant talking, regressing to her earlier pattern. At the same time, her junior high school educable mentally retarded class was mainstreamed for some academic classes, such as math, science, and English. This meant that the developmentally disabled adolescents had to take part in regular classes. This was a dreadful mistake for Polly, who could not adjust to the higher behavioral and academic expectations of the teacher. She was treated for two years by a pediatrician and a psychiatrist to help her adjust, but in the end her behavior in class and at home became so intolerable that her doctors asked that she be removed from academic mainstreaming. She stayed in regular classes for physical education, choir, home economics, and music, however, where she was able to do well and was pleased and satisfied with herself.

Until Polly reached her middle teens, she continued to suffer from incidents of violent behavior, although these were never as extreme as the ones she had experienced earlier. She received psychotherapy during two periods in her life, as a young child and between the ages of twelve and fourteen. She was on several medications until the age of fifteen but then was taken off medication entirely.

Polly made the transition from a self-contained educable mentally retarded junior high classroom into the special education section of the high school. What this meant was that she now had to negotiate corridors, stairways, and doors all day long as she went from class to class. The toughest part in learning her way around the big building was the adjustment to an individual program. She could not rely on a group to help her move between classes. The program she was in varied: Mondays, Wednesdays, and Fridays for certain classes; Tuesdays and Thursdays for others. On top of the physical difficulties, she and her developmentally disabled classmates had to learn to adhere to a schedule and be responsible for themselves in every way. Polly's teacher said that she went over this for four or five weeks with the whole class each morning. Polly reacted to the change with only moderately upset behavior—whining, crying, constant talking—and within three weeks had mastered both the building and her schedule. Her excessive talking moderated within two months, and by the second year she was much more comfortable.

At the high school, Polly stayed the same academically,

continuing to work between a second-grade and third-grade level. She did well in music and cooking but could do little if any sewing. The school's overall goal was to equip the developmentally handicapped students with the skills for basic survival, to get them to read on at least a functional level, and to teach them simple, job-related math. These students were also introduced to vocational training at the Connecticut Association for Retarded Adults's local greenhouse and tearoom. Polly's greatest talents and strengths showed up in the area of her job. By graduation, she was working daily as a waitress in the tearoom. Her ability to handle responsibility and, usually, to remain calm under pressure were surprising and remarkable. She was efficient and a good organizer.

Polly astonished many people by her success at the tearoom. She worked at the cash register (under supervision) and did well at it. She was also successful in another unexpected area, athletics. She developed her athletic ability late but applied herself well and won a gold medal in the 100-yard dash and a silver medal in the girls' relay in the Connecticut Special Olympics. She was one of their best swimmers and baseball pitchers.

Polly graduated from high school in June 1979 at twenty. After graduation, she and four others from her class were taken on a trip to Washington, D.C. Later that summer, she was one of five from her class chosen for training for a community job sponsored by the Association for Retarded Adults. The training took place at a special summer camp for the handicapped. At the end of the summer, Polly started work in a local restaurant, where she was in charge of making salads.

Polly was a good worker, and by and large retained control of herself. Nevertheless, as with many developmentally disabled persons, there were times when she lost control. Once, for instance, she found her way blocked in a kitchen aisle by two employees, who, busy talking, did not move to one side. After saying "Excuse me" once or twice, Polly went past, unintentionally shoving one of the employees. When she was reprimanded for this rudeness, Polly exploded and threw herself backward onto the red-hot stove-top grill. She was saved from being severely burned by the other terrified employees, but it took them half an hour to calm her hysterics.

Later Polly worked in another restaurant as a waitress. Her boss there was very pleased and regarded her as quick, capable, and responsible. The customers apparently liked her friendliness and her ability as a waitress. At this restaurant, Polly was in charge of food preparation for the following day. She was responsible for getting out the big cans of basic ingredients for the soups on the day's menu, and getting the elements for various salads ready and placed in the refrigerator. She was given more accountability and independence at this restaurant than at her previous job, and she responded well to the challenge. She appeared to perform better in a smaller, more individually run organization, working with only four or five others, than in the large restaurant sponsored by her Association for Retarded Adults.

Originally, just after graduation from high school, Polly's intention (and that of her family) was for her to live in a group home. After five years of waiting, however, she still had not been placed in one. She had been offered the opportunity to share an apartment with a male roommate, but her parents had turned this down because she lacked the training for independent living (grocery shopping, managing a checkbook, etc.) that is usually obtained by living in a group home first. The state had overlooked this essential step. In fact, Polly and her family were also aghast at the thought of a male roommate.

Polly still lives at home, and her mother still has to drive her to and from work. This is a considerable burden for Mrs. Daniels, but the walk to the bus from Polly's house is a mile along the edge of the road, not on a sidewalk. Mrs. Daniels doesn't feel that Polly is yet up to dealing with that every day.

Polly's future, as with all of the children discussed in this book, is uncertain (see p. 96). In 1992, Polly was told that she should be in a group home within a year. This seems optimistic in view of the pressure to put deinstitutionalized people in them first. If Polly gets into a group home, she would stay there one or two years and then, if all goes well, move into a supervised apartment. Her ability to advance in her job is understandably limited, but based on her past job performance and her proven efficiency, she might be able to become an assistant manager in a restaurant.

Of all the children described in this book, Polly's developmental course has remained the most perplexing to the professionals who worked with her. Had Polly's pervasive developmental disorder been more clearly defined initially thirty years ago and the work with her and her parents started earlier, she might have advanced farther than she has. This is, of course, unknowable. But over the years, mental health professionals and teachers who have known her have come to believe that she has unreleased potential for growth and adaptation.

This is the dichotomy in Polly's case, and perhaps the tragedy too. She has been more adaptable than expected—that is, she has always been able to accommodate herself to new people and surroundings. And, perhaps most touching of all, she is very aware of her situation and able to refer to herself as retarded. When asked how she feels about this, she says, "It makes me sad. I get very angry sometimes because I can't do things. I cry a lot. I cry when I see my friends cry, too."

As an adult, Polly has lost the china-doll fragility and white-and-pink prettiness of her childhood. She stands five feet two inches tall, and her ample figure requires careful dieting to keep trim. Unchanged are her flashing blue eyes and radiant smile, as are her tenseness and air of being in charge. Her good looks are marred by her prominent teeth, which, uncorrected by braces, have distorted the shape of her mouth and given a receding appearance to her jaw.

In October 1987, when she was tested at the Yale Child Study Center, Polly was twenty-eight. The psychologist described her as extremely cooperative and appropriate in her range of affects. She told the psychologist spontaneously about her job, and asked if the psychologist had met one of her friends, who was also being evaluated. It was interesting that she appeared to have some difficulty descending a ramp to the testing room, and perhaps this is a continuing indication of a degree of perceptual handicap.

WAIS-R
Verbal IQ: 63   Performance IQ: 62   Full Scale IQ: 61

VINELAND

Domain	Standard Score	Adaptive Level	Age Equivalent
Communication:	36	Low	7 yrs. 7 mos.
Daily Living:	85	Adequate	14 yrs. 9 mos.
Socialization:	59	Low	10 yrs. 4 mos.
Adaptive Behavior Composite:	55	Low	10 yrs. 11 mos.

ABC
49: Probably not autistic

In the Wechsler Adult Intelligence Scale-Revised (WAIS-R), Polly achieved a full-scale IQ score of 61, in the mildly retarded range. Within her performance scale IQ score of 62, she showed relative strength on a test for the ability to copy symbols paired with numbers, demonstrating an aptitude for learning unfamiliar tasks. Polly has speed and accuracy in visual motor coordination.

On the Vineland Adaptive Behavior Scale, Polly's composite score, including communication, daily living skills, and socialization, was 55. This was in the low range compared to all the adults in her peer group. She showed weakness in communication and strength in daily living skills. But compared with mentally retarded adults in nonresidential facilities, Polly's score was in the above-average range. Her maladaptive behaviors were biting her nails, being extremely anxious, having tic-like movements, and having trouble with concentration and attention.

One of the psychologists at the Yale Child Study Center, Alice Carter, had this to say about Polly's Vineland scores:

> It is striking that she continues to have difficulty in communication skills. She is on a fourth grade level in reading, alphabetizing, and writing. In socialization, she is functioning in the mild deficit range. This is good adaptation comparatively. Her daily living skills are in the adequate range compared to her normal peers.

"I spent all day trying to restrain her . . ."
by Jane Daniels

At 3:30 each afternoon, a blonde whirlwind enters our home. Her exuberance is overwhelming. She's so full of news that she's fairly bursting. At five feet two inches tall, she's about ten pounds overweight—ten pounds of solid muscle. Her figure is full-blown, a fact that makes her quite self-conscious. Her blue eyes sparkle, twinkle, and miss absolutely nothing. As she starts filling me in, in minute detail, about her fascinating day, I recall those uneasy first few years of Polly's life.

Childhood to 1976

Polly was born October 16, 1959. After a calm and uneventful pregnancy, her easy birth, with little or no labor, came as no surprise. She was a lovely, compact baby, the delight of the hospital nursery. She weighed seven pounds two ounces and was just eighteen inches long. I must admit that Tom and I were delighted to have such an adorable, placid infant. My son Jim, at three years old, was hell on wheels. And Danny, at just a year, took up most of my time.

Polly's first year was routine and uneventful. She turned over, sat up, crawled, and walked on the same timetable as the boys. However, there was one huge difference: She made not a sound. No, that's not quite accurate. She cried, or softly wept. But the cooings, gurglings, normal attempts at sounds were strangely absent. By the time she was two years old, I was constantly questioning her physician about her silence. His answer was always the same: "Why should she talk with four people to wait on her?" Polly's silence was accompanied by the most passive behavior I've ever seen. She never objected when Jimmy or Danny took her toys, or if she was trampled in play.

In fact, she never objected to anything. She remained perfectly calm, quiet, and unruffled, perfectly willing to be a spectator, always sitting in her stroller or on a lap and watching.

By the time Polly was two-and-a-half, I was distraught. She still had made no attempts at speech, not even a "da-da." Because of her silence, we were forced to play dangerous guessing games when illness struck. And Polly was plagued by colds and earaches. It was becoming frightening. I instinctively knew something was very wrong, but still her doctors laughed at my concern.

One spring morning, when Polly was three-and-a-half years old, I was awakened by a tap on the forehead (Polly's favorite method of awakening us), and a small, totally unfamiliar voice said, "I'm thirsty. May I have a drink?" I was stunned. Here she stood, thirty inches high, speaking for the first time, and in a sentence. I can still recall how excited we all were. Grandparents, friends, and neighbors were called, and everyone breathed a sigh of relief. We were all sure that the doctors were right. Polly hadn't spoken simply because she had nothing to say.

Our excitement and pleasure lasted for about one week. It became quickly evident that Polly had gone to the opposite end of the spectrum. For three years we had despaired of ever hearing her voice, and now we heard little else. Where or how Polly found her voice we'll never know. But once found, it's never been lost. Perhaps, in her innermost mind, she's afraid if she does stop talking her voice will disappear again. For whatever reason, Polly talks day and night, awake and asleep, right through TV programs, school, workshop, movies, records, and church—Polly TALKS!

The one constant thing we've all asked of Polly is to please be quiet. And it's the one thing she cannot do. Isn't it ironic that three years of worry and prayer should turn out like this?

It became evident, at the same time, that Polly had learned

something else along with speech. And that was fear. It became an integral part of Polly's character. She was terrified of noises. She even heard noises no one else did. A fire siren would send her screaming with her hands over her ears. The twelve o'clock whistle was a daily trauma. A dog barking would make her scream. A truck coming near on a street would make her freeze in her tracks. She could not maneuver steps without crawling up on her hands and knees. Approaching a doorway, she gave the impression of being blind, and she'd put her hands out in front of her to feel the emptiness. If she ran, she fell. So, with the sudden freedom of speech came terror.

When she was almost five, it became suddenly evident that Polly had lost her hearing, and for once the doctors agreed. They say it never rains but it pours—well, it sure poured all over us. Polly was due at the hospital for a tonsillectomy on May 10. On May 5, she became very ill with a strep throat. On May 7, we were told she had scarlet fever. She was given massive doses of penicillin, and she responded well. At seven o'clock on the evening of May 9, Polly's dad became violently ill, so ill, in fact, that he was put to bed for three weeks with an acute gall bladder infection and ordered not to get up.

Polly and I left at noon on Thursday, May 10, to register her at the hospital for a series of misadventures not to be believed. The first problem was simple—no bed. A small child had been waiting for six hours to be picked up and brought home. And no one had come. Polly and I waited in the play-room. By eight o'clock that night Polly was in her room and becoming more and more apprehensive (which always increases her perseveration).

I stayed with Polly until she fell asleep, and then, on the advice of her doctor, I left for home and my sick husband. The other two mothers in the room offered to look after Polly should she awaken during the night. Her doctor said Polly was scheduled for surgery at 8 A.M. and he would call me at home by 11 A.M. and tell me when I could see her.

I'll never forget how the minutes crawled by the next day. When the phone remained silent until afternoon, I nearly lost my mind. At 2 P.M., they called to tell me that she was just out of surgery and in recovery. It seems they had prepped and medicated her for surgery at 6:30 A.M., then someone realized that they hadn't done a blood-clotting time. Surgery was delayed until 11 A.M. but no further medication was given.

The mothers in her room filled me in about Polly's terrified screaming and fantastic attempts to run away. They told me that orderlies and interns had to come from all over the hospital to restrain her. Polly was carried screaming into surgery. I heard all of this with a sinking heart, not knowing what would come down from the recovery room. It was more than an hour before they brought her down to me, a tiny, pathetic waif covered from head to toe with blood. They "allowed" me to clean her up.

When Polly was completely out from under the effects of the anesthesia, she tried, even though her throat ached, to talk. It was awful. The stuttering and stammering startled us both. I took Polly home as soon as possible and tried to comfort her, reassure her, and love her—to try in every way to erase the painful memories the hospital had left.

Polly's behavior for the next year was impossible. Her pent-up fury spilled over everywhere. Her nonstop talking irritated everyone. Her perseveration became so overwhelming that I counted the same question asked forty-five times in sixty minutes. Through all this she continued to stutter and stammer. However, her fears seemed to vanish in the face of this rage.

When Polly was five, we were advised by her doctors not to have any guests in our home, not even relatives. This went on for two years, and then the grandparents were finally allowed to visit. But for two more years no friends of the boys' or of ours were allowed in our home. Polly's whole sense of being and security was tied up in me and our home. She became very threatened when someone outside of our family entered, or at least this is what we were told.

How detrimental this has been to us all! It became a habit always to be alone. It was unhealthy and cruel, to say the least. It has been difficult for both Tom and me to combat the feelings of frustration and disappointment we experienced when our friends forgot us. I find, even now, that Tom is cynical in his approach to people. He tends to embrace such solitary hobbies as painting and sailing.

It took quite a few years to convince our boys that they could bring friends home. I had to devote my absolute attention to Polly while any stranger was in our home. But it was worth it to know the boys' friends were welcome.

When Polly was six, we were finally referred to the local hospital's child psychiatric unit on a six-week emergency-treatment basis. Because of the uniqueness of Polly's problems, she continued to be treated there for three years. She spent the last year in a special nursery class where she could be observed. During all three years she was seen twice a week by a leading child psychiatrist. Unfortunately, this doctor could not or would not have any dealing with the parents. Therefore I was again ignored when I expressed alarm over the new and destructive behavior I was seeing at home. I spent my time with a social worker trying to learn how to live and cope with Polly.

Her tantrums were becoming more and more violent. It is horrifying for a mother to watch an adorable, petite (at six years old, Polly was barely three feet tall) child attempt to strangle a beloved pet or deliberately pull the wings off flies and butterflies. We listened to her plead with us to hurt her, and we listened to the terrified screams all night from nightmares she couldn't or wouldn't remember.

It was heartbreaking to hear Jim and Danny beg me each

morning to protect their dog from Polly and not let her hurt me either. We sent Jim and Danny away each weekend to stay with their grandparents to give them some relief from the continual screaming, kicking, and throwing things. This tiny, adorable child was destroying my home right under my eyes, and I was powerless to stop her.

A climax came in June of that year. Danny and Jim left on Friday afternoon to stay with Grandma, and Tom was away working the whole weekend. I was left alone with Polly. She had lost all control. She broke two windows, three lamps, a table, and many odds and ends. She then tried to get scissors or a knife to use on herself. I spent all of Saturday and Saturday evening fighting to restrain her. Both she and I fell asleep on the floor from sheer exhaustion, but at 3:30 Sunday morning, I heard her muttering and found her again trying to get some-thing with which to hurt herself. I spent Sunday morning restraining what was now a small, furious, soiled, screaming animal.

By knocking the phone off the hook, I managed to call the operator, and she contacted the doctor. Within half an hour, both my pediatrician and Polly's psychiatrist were at the house. Polly was given a shot to knock her out and was stripped, bathed, and put to bed. The pediatrician and I had furious words with the psychiatrist, who admitted he had seen this breakdown coming and, in fact, had promoted it. He had allowed and encouraged these episodes because he thought it was the only way to break through the wall Polly had erected. He obviously did not believe in considering the effects his therapy might have on the rest of the family. The consequences of what he had done were disastrous.

I would not allow them to take Polly to the hospital, although I now realize that I was in no condition to make any decision at all. Polly was given massive doses of Thorazine daily. I lost fifteen pounds in two weeks, and her brothers were nervous and frightened. The whole episode seemed to break something within Polly, and she, seemingly overnight, reverted to a confused, frightened, insecure little waif.

At the time this was happening, Jim was nine years old and Danny was seven. Danny is very quiet, shy, and almost withdrawn. Jim is quick, aggressive, and slightly hostile. Danny's stuttering and Jim's asthma may or may not be attributed to Polly, but the fact remains that both boys were severely affected and needed professional help. My husband was sick over money, and so was I. Financially, we were sunk. Polly's expenses had been appalling. Her doctors, special nursery schools, and medications had come close to ruining us. I could not work because I had to drive Polly to the Ives preschool and back each morning. Add all of this to the burden of worry we carried, and it's a wonder we survived.

But survive we did. Jim and Danny's relationships with Polly have never been good. Now that they are adults, they have told me that they lived in constant fear that Polly would physically harm me or that I would crack up under the strain—a fearful way to grow up.

Things began to change for the better. Polly entered the Ives preschool for special children when she was six and stayed a year, until she had turned eight. The hours were 9 to 11 each morning. Polly spent school time with four patient and understanding teachers at the Ives preschool. At this point in her life, her gross-motor control was fair; her fine-motor control was horrible. She had *no* depth perception. Her spatial relationships were poor, her sense of self nil, and so on. The head teacher gave Polly her first taste of classroom structure and discipline. I made many trips to the school to pick up Polly and bring her home in the middle of the morning when she was dismissed early for being overly disruptive. The teacher would give her three chances to behave, then call me. I never needed to say a word to Polly. In her eyes, being sent home from school was the worst punishment ever. And she improved quickly. At eight, Polly was allowed to join the public school system and spent half-days in a learning disability class. When she was nine, our town decided to try her in an all-day educable mentally retarded class.

The years between nine and twelve were relatively uneventful. Polly adjusted well to the educable mentally retarded class, although her relationships with peers were poor then and are not much better now. However, she related beautifully to her teachers. This has been a pattern with Polly.

But when Polly was twelve, she had two setbacks. Just as she entered puberty, her paternal grandparents retired to Arizona for six months of every year. She was very close to them. She had spent much time with them and loved them dearly, and she reacted to their absence much as a small child reacts to a death in the family. Her feelings of anger and rejection spilled over everywhere. Her behavior started to break down at an appalling rate—there seemed to be little we could do to help her.

At the same time, Polly became caught up in a new and, for her, tragic mess at school called "mainstreaming." For some academic subjects, she was put in the same class as "normal" children her age. It was hard to believe that any professional could expect a child with an IQ of 61 and a second-grade performance level to be comfortable in an eighth-grade math class. I repeatedly tried to convince the authorities that Polly was breaking down under the strain caused by academic mainstreaming, but it wasn't until the fall of the year she was fourteen that her classroom behavior became as intolerable as her behavior at home.

We took Polly to a very expensive child psychiatrist out of sheer desperation. At fourteen, Polly was five feet two inches tall and weighed about 115 pounds. When she threw a tantrum or, worse, pulled down that invisible curtain that shut out sight and sound, I had to subdue her physically. It was becoming nearly impossible. The constant battles were wearing us all down. Again Jim and Danny became very concerned about me, and we were torn about the real possibility that Polly might have to be put in a residential school.

The prescription from this child psychiatrist was that Polly *must* be removed from regular classroom academics and only mainstreamed in nonacademic subjects. The following year she went to the high school educable mentally retarded class with some mainstreaming in the morning and an area services workshop in the afternoon. The remainder of that first year was a nightmare, but Polly responded, and the next year was worth waiting for.

Things began to stabilize a bit. Jim, Danny, and I spent a year examining our feelings at a counseling center. It helped us all tremendously. Polly adored the high school, and she was so relaxed at home it was like having a different child around. She was very successful at the workshop and loved going. She was trained in food services that spring and afterward worked as a waitress in a tearoom operated by the workshop. She was very proud of her paycheck and knew she had earned every cent of it.

When our eldest son decided to get married, he became very concerned about having children. I felt that this was a realistic concern, and we spent six months going to a genetic clinic. I'm afraid their results were not as definite as I would have liked. The conclusion was that Polly was mildly retarded; she was classified as "moderately educable mentally retarded." The results also described her as severely learning disabled, and no genetic reason could be found for either condition. We decided that Jim and Danny had every bit as good a chance of having normal babies as anyone else.

By seventeen, Polly had leveled off intellectually. As a parent, it's hard to accept the fact that your daughter will never progress beyond the second-grade performance level she achieved at that age (she was tested every year), but as an educator I'm thankful she had seventeen years before reaching that plateau.

Polly spent three years at the high school, with half-days in her educable mentally retarded class and half-days at the workshop. When she was through at the high school, she was twenty. She remained at the workshop facility and trained to have a simple job in the community while she worked there. By the time she was twenty-four or twenty-five, we hoped there would be group housing available for the retarded in our community. I wanted to see Polly living and working as independently as is possible for her. Perhaps then we could begin to live without tension and dread hanging over our heads.

Adulthood, 1976 to 1986

Ten years later, Tom and I are now in our mid-fifties and Polly is twenty-seven. The changes in Polly's life, and therefore in ours, can only be measured in inches since she graduated from high school.

Polly is now an attractive, slender young woman—tense, nervous, obviously unsure of herself in any new situation. She still relates poorly to her age group but very well to very young children or elderly people.

She is still home with us, but her brothers no longer live at home. Jim is married and has a child. Danny is single and lives alone, but both boys have chosen "helping" professions: one is in social work; the other is a teacher. Interesting that the siblings of so many handicapped people choose to devote their lives to helping others.

Polly has been at the head of a waiting list for a group home for six years. However, because federal and state funding for group homes is being cut year after year, applicants are chosen on basis of need. As it stands now, one of us or both of us must die, or we must in some way abuse Polly, in order to get her into a group home.

"Change." That word looms very large in my mind. Polly reacts to, resents, and resists change in any form—changes in people, places, jobs. Even changes in furniture or draperies upset her. The changes that normally take place in a family cannot take place in the family of an autistic adult. The freedom that Tom and I should be experiencing now, after raising our family, is not there. We must always plan around Polly's schedule. We must always take her with us on trips, because she cannot stay alone. We have no quiet times to reflect and discuss things because she is always there. And she talks and talks and talks.

Polly still works in the restaurant owned by the area sheltered workshop. She has had success as a waitress and now as an assistant cook. Until recently, her work hours were the same as her father's. Now she works from 2 P.M. to 10 P.M., which leaves us time alone in the evening, and I do appreciate that. But like most things to do with Polly, we take two steps forward and one step backward. This new schedule also means that I have Polly alone with me all day, every day. And ironically, while I now have a few hours alone with Tom, I'm so exhausted from spending my days with Polly's anxieties and constant perseveration, that I can barely function.

Polly's new hours now include Friday and Saturday nights. Do I tell Tom I can't go camping weekends because I must wait for Polly to get home from work? Or do I go camping, hand Polly a key, and say, "See you in three days. Good luck"? How can I leave her alone when I know full well that an emergency, no matter how small, will send her right over the edge, and that small, persistent voice inside me asks, Will that be the time she can't come back?

Privacy in our home is at a premium. A quiet request, asking Polly to leave us alone for a few minutes, is viewed by her as rejection. She insists on staying in the room for any and all phone calls.

Somehow, although none of these behaviors is new, all seem harder and harder for me to deal with. I enjoyed raising my children, but I did look forward to the day they'd be out on their own, and Tom and I would again be a couple. By and large, however, for most of us with handicapped children, the natural course of events—children growing up and leaving home—will not take place. Perhaps, someday, this will be addressed by the professionals. There is a need—*I* have a need.

Postscript (1992), by Virginia Sperry

The situation at the Daniels home is still unchanged. Polly continues to work happily (and successfully) at the same restaurant. She lives at home, with—still—no prospect of a move to a group home. Recently Mrs. Daniels was notified that there was an opening for Polly in an apartment, with a young man as an apartment mate. To discuss this possibility, a meeting was held, attended by Mr. and Mrs. Daniels, other parents of girls also being considered for this opening, and the professionals in authority. The apartment was geographically too far away from Polly's job, and the young man, in a wheelchair because of spina bifida, presented a problem for Polly, who insisted on sharing living space only with another woman. Mr. and Mrs. Daniels explained both obstacles: Polly loved her job and did not want to change it, and she was frightened of sharing an apartment with a young man. The Danielses felt encouraged that "this time" (Mrs. Daniels's words), the professionals heard their needs and understood the family situation.

Mrs. Daniels says that she now accepts that Polly will probably never have the opportunity to live in either a group home or a supervised apartment. She describes herself as angry and embittered but resigned.

Although Polly remains at home, Mrs. Daniels has managed to achieve some life on her own. Always musical, she has a small organ at home, as well as a portable organ. Since 1986, she has developed a business of providing music, accompanied by a guitarist, at parties and restaurants. This is certainly an outlet, allowing her some time away from home and Polly's constant demands.

Mrs. Daniels is still fearful of leaving Polly alone, and justifiably so. Recently Polly was at home while Mrs. Daniels took one of her dogs to the veterinarian, thinking she would be gone from the house an hour. During this hour, a severe, unexpected thunderstorm (with lightning) developed. When Mrs. Daniels arrived home and called out, "Polly, we're home," there was no answer. In a state of panic, she ran to Polly's room to find Polly curled up in a fetal position, frozen. Mrs. Daniels soothed her, comforted her, to no avail. Only after several hours did Polly come out of this state of petrified fear and finally talk about the storm. It is this sort of thing Mrs. Daniels had in mind when she said her daughter might go over the edge and never come back. And it is exactly the possibility of such a thing occurring that keeps her chained to her home, and to Polly.

Postscript (1995)

There is a happier ending. Polly now lives in a supervised condominium, goes independently on the bus to work, manages her checkbook, banking, and day-to-day living successfully. This bears out the assessment that all along Polly had great (undeveloped) potential.

4 • THE CHILD FANTASIST: BILL KOLINSKI
born January 17, 1963

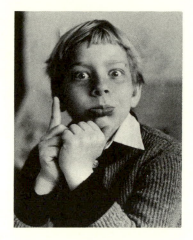

Bill came to Ives from public school kindergarten. A teacher from Ives was asked to observe him in the kindergarten to see if the Ives program was appropriate for him. According to his school social worker, Bill had been in trouble from his first day at school because of his behavior, which was so disruptive that his teacher could no longer manage him and still teach twenty other children.

Bill would walk up and down the aisles, sometimes running all around the room. He often babbled nonsense syllables. Even when he talked understandably, he would suddenly break off and chant. As he ran up and down the aisles, he would lightly tap a classmate with his hand or, occasionally, a workbook. He sat down when told to by the teacher but was soon up again, wandering once more. There were angry, protesting murmurs from the other children, but Bill appeared as unconnected with the reality of the classroom around him as a cloud floating by. It was easy to see why he could not be contained in a public school setting, and to understand why the children teased him unmercifully.

The teacher reported that Bill was hard to manage in many other ways. When he was willing to stay in his seat, he refused to follow general classroom instructions unless convinced by the teacher that it was important. At home, if Bill misbehaved, he was so sensitive that a look of disapproval from his mother was sufficient to discipline him. Sensitive and shy, he would also run away and hide, or at least refuse to speak, if there were visitors in the house.

Ives accepted Bill into its program provided that he be evaluated first by the consulting specialist at the Yale Child Study Center. Like most parents who have sustained the shock of discovering their child is "different," Bill's parents had not yet come to terms with his condition. They came to visit Ives, bringing Bill along. His father, a chemical engineer, was a reticent man, but he listened with intelligent and concerned interest to the discussion of the school. Bill's mother, in contrast, was outgoing. She smiled warmly, and she asked most of the questions. Both parents explained Bill's strange behavior by saying, "Bill marches to his own tune. He does not join in the children's playing because he is too bright and too grown-up."

Their visit to Ives only half-persuaded them that Bill might benefit from the change, and only reluctantly did they sign the consent form for him to undergo developmental and psychometric testing at the Yale Child Study Center.

Bill was almost seven years old when he was tested. He had been told by his mother that the testing was important, so he was cooperative. His performance on the Stanford-Binet Intelligence Scale yielded an IQ score of 94, placing him in the low-average range. He did very well on rote learning and memory items, scoring as high as the nine-year-old level. This suggested that through special help in dealing with his short attention span, his problems with distinguishing fantasy from reality, and his difficulty with logical thinking, he could function intellectually at a fully average level. He had some additional symptoms, however. He showed considerable discomfort in social interaction; he was very difficult to reassure and calm down when he was upset; and his speech evinced substantial problems in social and emotional development and functioning. Bill was often withdrawn and apparently preoccupied with ideas and fantasies that impelled him to bizarre behavior. Yale diagnosed him as having an atypical personality with autistic features.

The test results convinced Bill's parents that he needed different schooling, with small classes and more individual attention, and they chose to send Bill to the Ives preschool. He stayed three years.

During Bill's first year at Ives, he was withdrawn, physically awkward, rigid, and fearful. When he joined in play, he was a follower. He had trouble choosing which toy, which art material, which piece of outdoor equipment to use, but he liked to ride on the large toy trucks. His speech held many odd sounds, like "Boom!", "Bang!" and other sounds or words that appeared to have no reference to anything. Rather than answer a question directly, he would answer with an association which made sense to him but seemed farfetched or improbable to others. He could not distinguish between reality and fantasy. When he pretended to be a rabbit or an elephant in rhythm games or in acting out a story, he became so involved that he lost his awareness of the game and seemed to believe that he *was* the animal he was imitating.

The teachers at Ives worked with his illogical thought processes in many ways. They spent a good deal of time patiently untangling his confusion, for example, over how to see similarities in two different things, such as a plum and a peach. They showed him pictures of stuffed toys or, when possible, of real animals, saying, "This is a rabbit (or elephant), but you are Bill." They showed him at the same time in a long mirror that he was a boy, not an animal.

By the end of the first year, he had improved. His speech was more direct and meaningful. He was beginning to distinguish more clearly between what was real and what was fantasy. He liked outdoor play with one or two children at school, and he was playing at home with the neighborhood children.

By the end of his third year at Ives, Bill had improved dramatically. His bizarre behavior had almost disappeared. He was enthusiastic about physical activities, running relays, doing handstands, playing circle games. This new involvement and comfort showed in his swimming. Instead of clinging to a teacher or the side of the pool, he was swimming freely. He liked to bounce in the water, to put his head under the water, to sit-jump into the pool, to be involved in races and chase games with one child and a teacher.

Despite this improvement, however, Bill retained some fearfulness. He hated being splashed, was afraid of the water gushing from the side of the pool, and in general showed his sensitivity to and fear of the unknown. This was borne out in his social relationships. He approached cautiously any new or different situations or persons, asked a great many questions, and was only satisfied with a concrete answer or reassurance.

By the time he was nine, Bill met first-grade standards in all school subjects. He had developed writing ability in both stories and plays. He loved to draw maps of the streets in his town. He now walked, ran, jumped, and hopped more easily than he had before and seemed to have lost some of his prior awkwardness and clumsiness. His doctor thought that there had been some improvement in Bill's *neuromotor organization*. The specialist at the Yale Child Study Center, the Ives staff, and Mr. and Mrs. Kolinski agreed that Bill was ready to return gradually to the public school class.

At this time, Bill was also retested at the Yale Child Study Center. The testing confirmed the improvement in Bill's functioning on the Stanford-Binet Scale (he scored an IQ of 99), as well as the even more dramatic changes in his personality and behavior. The evaluation described him as less withdrawn, much less lost in fantasy, much more in touch with everyday events and people. His thinking was less rigid, his responsiveness to people more personalized, his general behavior less stereotypic than it was at age seven. While there remained some tendency to bottle up his feelings and, as his mother put it, "to cry inwardly," Bill had grown in his ability to say how he felt, and to respond to efforts to help him.

He still retained some literal-mindedness and a relative inflexibility, which showed itself in his failure to get the point of pranks, jokes, and incongruities. He expected things always to be logical and predictable and became confused when they were not. But unlike many autistic-like children, he was not attached to certain toys or books. The evaluators noted that he had a few obsessional preoccupations (such as mapmaking), but that these were not so totally involving as they had been earlier and could now be used as vehicles for learning. He continued to need help with adaptation to social groups and his relationship with his peers.

Starting in the spring of 1972, when he was nine, Bill attended the Ives preschool in the mornings and a regular third-grade class in the afternoons. At first one of his Ives teachers went with him, but as Bill became comfortable in his new setting, this stopped. That fall, he entered regular fourth grade. On the advice of Bill's public school social worker, one of his teachers at Ives visited his class several times during that fall to facilitate the transition for his teacher, Bill, and the rest of the class. This succeeded, and Bill was soon accepted by his classmates and was doing well in all subjects.

Years later, Bill reflected on his experience at Ives and the transition back to public school: "I didn't know that [Ives] was a special school. I liked it because there weren't many children, and I got a lot of attention. . . . I minded going back to third grade in public school because there were so many children."

Throughout public school, Bill did well, and he graduated at the age of eighteen. He had been particularly involved in the

drama club. He still could not talk about his feelings, and, at
one point, his social worker had recommended to him that he
see a psychiatrist. Bill, with his family's cooperation, had tried
this but felt that therapy had not helped. His own comment on
the experience, made several years later, was, "I didn't know
how to use it. I could use it now."

After high school, Bill enrolled in a local teachers' college.
He planned to major in drama with an emphasis on acting, but
also took courses in chemistry, English, psychology, math, and
speech in the theater and made grades in the As and Bs. He
lived in a house with boys on one floor and girls on another.
They all took turns at cooking, which Bill enjoyed, and had a
good deal of fun together. But hospitable and friendly as he
was, there was still a sensitive, wary, cautious quality in his
approach to people.

Bill graduated from college in June 1985 at twenty-two.
That summer, he went abroad with a student group and had a
wonderful time, yet at home he had no friends his own age. He
had majored, finally, in journalism, and minored in drama. He
worried, however, that the field of journalism was so competitive he would have a hard time starting a career.

After college, he worked in a fast-food restaurant and
went to classes in library science at night. After receiving some
job counseling, he changed his career goals and entered an out-
of-state culinary institute.

Between his first and second years at the culinary institute,
Bill once again traveled abroad, some of the time with a group,
and had visited his Polish relatives in Warsaw and attended the
university there. During the trip, he met an attractive American
girl who invited him to visit her in the Midwest, which he did
sometime later.

In summer 1987, Bill had three job offers from local
restaurants and chose the one with the busy lunch trade because
of its favorable downtown location. He became responsible for

the salad bar and used his mother's Polish salad recipes. His potato salad was considered special, as were his artistic decorations of the salad bar. He left this restaurant to go back to his last year of school with a letter of recommendation from his employer for a job well done.

By the fall of 1988, Bill was making the dean's list in school. He had a friend as a roommate, and they joined a church group that sponsored a senior citizens' camp. Bill and his friend went there on weekends to cook. He also had a part-time job in the cafeteria of the institute.

At twenty-five, Bill had matured. The tentative, shy, and hesitant quality of his speech and manner had been replaced by a self-confident directness. His voice was deeper, and although he occasionally seemed to hesitate over certain words, he spoke with assurance and decisiveness.

Bill's strength is in his verbal ability. He beats everyone at games such as Trivial Pursuit. According to his mother, "He seems to know it all," but she remains concerned that his slow, deliberate approach to problems or to work might handicap him.

Bill now works at Disney World in Florida. He had been nervous at first about moving but found a nice apartment and bought a used car. He sent a postcard of "Main Street, U.S.A." to one of his old teachers, describing his new job working "for the Mouse" (as he put it). His boyhood physician at Yale read the postcard with a smile, saying, "How nice! He's really succeeding, isn't he?"

As an adult, Bill has achieved a degree of independence rare among autistic people. He started out with several advantages: a basic intelligence, good health, and parents who supported and encouraged him at every stage. The one-to-one teaching he received from ages six to nine at Ives (when he was phased back into public school) gave him a sound academic first-through-second-grade foundation and helped him overcome his confusion between fantasy and reality. Last, but far from least, it enhanced his ability to relate to both adults and peers so that he could return to public school.

At the age of twenty-four, Bill achieved the following scores during the October 1987 testing at Yale Child Study Center. Bill's mother answered the questions on the Vineland Adaptive Behavior Scale.

WAIS-R
Verbal IQ: 103   Performance IQ: 85   Full Scale IQ: 94

Vineland

Domain	Standard Score	Adaptive Level	Age Equivalent
Communication:	97	Adequate	17 yrs. 9 mos.
Daily Living:	108	Adequate	18 yrs. 11 mos.
Socialization:	74	Moderately low	13 yrs. 9 mos.
Adaptive Behavior Composite:	90	Low	12 yrs. 5 mos.

ABC
63: Possibly autistic

The following is a discussion of the results abstracted from the report of testing:

> Behaviorally, Bill appeared extremely anxious, clearing his throat and stuttering; his face was flushed. During the Object Assembly task, he manipulated one puzzle piece for three minutes unsuccessfully. He achieved a score in the superior range on a verbal task administered in a subsequent session (because of the shortage of time) *over the telephone*. The psychologist commented: "It is unclear whether or not the interpersonal distance of the telephone minimized Bill's anxiety and enhanced his performance."

On the WAIS-R, Bill's Full Scale IQ score was 94, in the average range of intellectual functioning. There was a significant difference of eighteen points between his verbal scale score of 103 and his performance scale score of 85. Bill, in short, is stronger in verbal expression and comprehension than in nonverbal visual–spatial tasks. He showed relative strength in abstract verbal reasoning (similarities) [i.e., how are a dog and a cat alike?].

On the Vineland Adaptive Behavior Scale, Bill obtained a composite score of 90. This covered communication, daily living skills, and socialization. He is in the average range when compared to "normal" adults in his peer group. He showed significant strengths in daily living skills and weakness in socialization. Maladaptive behaviors included poor eye control, occasional anxiety, overdependency [i.e., on other people for initiatives], and difficulty with concentration.

In 1995, Bill feels that he has grown out of autism. Unlike the other individuals portrayed here, he is able to regard himself and assess his life, often eloquently. Bill's perspective on his autistic beginnings is given in Appendix A.

"He wrote a book himself..."
by Fran Kolinski

Bill lives in Orlando, Florida, now. He went to a culinary institute in Rhode Island, and when he graduated, he was offered a job at Disney World. He has a new apartment and is very friendly with some people there who are almost like second parents to him. He bought a car, and he seems to enjoy himself.

Bill was going to be a chef when he went there, but they thought he was too slow for that, so he was made assistant chef. He helps the chef by preparing salad, dessert, and hors d'œuvres. He's also partly responsible for ordering food. He has to keep a list of what they need, and he has to store it and make sure the supplies are all there. I think it bothers him that he is not a full chef yet, but he really doesn't know what to do about it.

Bill surprised us at Christmas with a book he wrote himself—a history of our family entitled *The Branches of a Proud Tree*. He gave every member of our family a copy. In it he talks a lot about himself and a lot about his brother Steve, who is his idol. Bill has done many things in his life just to prove that he could do the same things Steve did. His brother went to Europe; Bill went to Europe. Steve learned to ski; Bill went skiing. Bill is very honest in what he writes, for instance, that Steve was successful in school and that he, Bill, was not that good. He doesn't try to make himself look good and he writes exactly what he feels.

In Florida, Bill has joined a church group and has mentioned something about being born again. They seem to have a nice group of young people and they help Bill a lot. Just before Christmas this year they put on a play, which they performed at several different churches. Bill had a small role, but he gave so much emotion to his part that people came up to him and asked him if he was interested in performing professionally. I think he likes acting so much because on stage he can forget that he is Bill Kolinski and be somebody else.

I can't remember when I first heard the word "autistic". Bill was having trouble in kindergarten. My husband and I met with his teachers, and they advised us to try a special school for Bill. At the meeting my husband got kind of upset. He said, "There's nothing wrong with Bill." But they explained their concerns to us, and we realized that there was more to it than Bill's being just a little shy, different, or slow in maturing. He did things that were different from what other kids did. For instance, when Bill was four or five, he started touching people. Without any reason, at kindergarten and at home, he would get up when everyone else was sitting down. If he didn't feel like sitting down, he would get up and start touching people. We would say, "Bill, don't do that." Then he would get a kind of stupid grin on his face. We never asked anyone about it because we didn't really think there was anything wrong. He also would sit in front of a record player just watching the turntable going around and around. He could sit for an hour and just stare at that. A normal child would never do that. After Bill started school at Ives, we were told autistic children are fascinated by movement.

He's better now, but even when he comes home for a visit, if I ask him the wrong question, a little too close to what he doesn't want to talk about, he won't answer or say anything; he'll just stare away into space. Now I just walk away and say, "It doesn't make any difference," and after two minutes he's normal again.

In his book, Bill writes about Ives. He states that he asked me once when he started school why he went there, and I said, "Bill, you were kind of silly and bothered the kids in the other school and they didn't like that, and you do better in a smaller group." He writes that he needed a one-to-one situation where a teacher could concentrate on him. That must still be what he believes; it was also true, and Ives made a great deal of difference in Bill's education. When he left Ives for the third grade, he never missed a class.

Bill tests as a perfectly normal person, and throughout school he always made at least Bs and Cs. He still has autistic behaviors, though, and they reach into his performance. It's hard to describe; he's almost normal. But something always seems to be there to hold him back.

Compared to "normal" kids growing up—getting fresh, disobeying parents, not having any respect, etc.—Bill was always a pleasure to be with. He was a little bit slow and a little bit strange sometimes, but he was always a joy. He was loving, in his own way. He never came out and put his arms around us, but we never had any feeling that he was unaffectionate.

Bill is shy. Even now, I think he gets lost in a big group. You have to address him personally; otherwise, he is not a person to come up to you. When someone wants to hug him, he used to put a stop to it, but now he is much better. I was surprised when I visited him in Florida. We went to a restaurant, and he said to me, "I'm always telling you about this girl. I want you to meet her. She's coming over, and she's having a cup of coffee with us." The girl was a very outgoing person. She came in the restaurant and said, "Oh, hi, Bill." And she hugged him and kissed him right in front of everybody, and he did the same thing, and I thought, "Oh, look at that!"

Our grandson, Robert, is only a few years younger than Bill, and they went to culinary school together. Robert arrived from high school and took the full four years to finish. Bill had gone to college and so was able to graduate in two years. I don't think Robert realizes that there is anything "wrong" with Bill. Just once in a while he gets impatient that Bill's not fast enough. Robert is kind of like the brother from the movie, *Rain Man*. He likes money—that type. They see each other at

Christmas, and he will tell Bill, "C'mon, you have to complain to your boss that you want a raise." And then Bill gets kind of scared and insecure. He doesn't really know what to answer. In one way he probably thinks that Robert is right, but he realizes that for him that's not the right thing to do.

Bill and I saw *Rain Man* together. I liked it and he loved it. Many of the things that Dustin Hoffman did reminded me of Bill, like the way he looked when people talked to him and he was daydreaming. All of a sudden he wasn't there. I asked Bill if he had heard of autism. I wondered if he ever had any suspicion that he was autistic. Even when he was at Ives, he always seemed to think that he wasn't really like the other children. He was more interested in what the people did that worked there. He once said to me, "I think when I grow up I would like to be a counselor like Mrs. Sperry to help these children." After he saw *Rain Man*, I asked him what he thought of it. He said, "Oh, that was a fantastic film." But he never said anything to suggest that he thought he was perhaps a little bit like that.

Of course, we are proud of him and happy for him. His happiness is most important. He is not that successful, but it's good enough for him. If lack of success made him unhappy, I would be concerned, but he does well enough and realizes that he cannot do more. And he is content enough. In general, I don't worry about him. We always think about the time when we are not here anymore, when he will have to take care of himself, but so far he is doing a good job.

Bill has never given us a reason to be angry at him. He has always been obedient and loving. It's almost like God giving us a special child to take care of, and it's a privilege for us to be able to do that.

5 • LACKING SPONTANEITY: DAVID ELLIS
born April 16, 1965

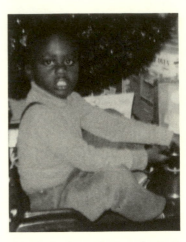

David was referred to Ives School in the spring of 1969 at age four. He had been regarded as perfectly normal until about age two, when his slow motor development and lack of speech began to concern his parents and pediatrician. He had asthma and recurrent ear infections, and often he had to be taken to the emergency room because of acute asthma and bronchitis attacks. Consequently, he was closely monitored by a pediatric team at the Yale-New Haven Hospital, where he was given a thorough physical. But no physical findings explained his delay and "differentness."

Before Ives, David was tested at the Yale Child Study Center. The evaluation showed that he was mildly retarded and possibly suffered from *aphasia*, a brain disorder in which the ability to use language is affected and sometimes totally absent or lost. But he was not easy to test on his developmental level. He had some success on nonverbal items at a three-year-old level. His language was the most delayed and consisted only of five words: "ball," "ookie," "key," "car," and "water." He also had superficial relationships with people and difficulty in coping with anxiety. His major handicaps were felt to be his social and verbal communication disorders. He also had difficulty with tasks requiring reasoning and visual-motor coordination.

The doctor who tested David said that he could not be

induced to use more than a few of the test materials. Outdoors, he ran around, chasing other children but never playing with them. At times, he appeared to try to cooperate during the session, but the doctor was never sure he understood words, although he was alert to sounds and followed a few directions when accompanied by gestures.

When David entered Ives, he was small for his age. His smile, shy yet expressing the desire to make contact, lit up his face and eyes. He held his body rigidly, approaching both people and activities with caution. The teachers saw him as "handsome, neat, clean, extremely quiet, unsure of himself, and lacking spontaneity."

In the beginning, David was fearful of all activities, but by June, after turning five, he had made real progress. He was jumping on the trampoline, riding in the wagon, and riding the tricycle. In the gym program, he was participating willingly in swimming. His end-of-the-year report from Ives said, "David has changed a great deal. He is trying to speak louder (he whispered in September). He is in a reading program and recognizes and understands twelve words, picking out the correct word to go with the right picture. He teases and even has some silly moods. All in all, he seems more relaxed and sure of himself."

David started speech therapy in his second year at Ives to help him overcome his lack of spontaneous speech. The therapist used a dollhouse, small dolls, and play furniture, and soon David could name all of them. The therapist said that his interest lay in things rather than in people. She said his visual memory seemed much better than his auditory memory, but that he soon learned to complete nursery rhymes by supplying the missing word. He responded to his name by echoing it. He wanted desperately to learn how to write it and worked on that daily with the therapist. He was made to look her in the eyes when he talked and to say his words clearly. This took much patient, firm repetition.

By the time he was six, David was talking so he could be understood. He no longer whispered or covered his eyes. He played with other children, although it was still more of a side-by-side play than a true give-and-take. He could even, on occasions, become gently aggressive.

After two years at the Ives preschool, David was ready to go on to the newly established public school program for developmentally disabled children and adolescents. There he went into the state-funded communication disorders program, where he learned sign language. He blossomed and began to make fantastic strides. From signing, he quickly progressed to talking, at first hesitantly and then quite fluently. He soon read, spelled, and wrote, although his teacher reported that he had some difficulty mastering verb tenses. The teacher also said he loved to read aloud, especially history.

The director of the program was enthusiastic as she talked about David. She emphasized the role his parents had played. They had been responsible, cooperative in every way, and caring of David.

Socially, however, David still had severe problems. He could not make changes easily, and he was still "remote" in his contacts with others. As with so many of these young people, he had trouble understanding emotions or making contact emotionally. He had some peculiar behavior traits as well, such as talking to himself, and he teased and taunted his peers, often without apparent reason. David also had temper tantrums, and it was often difficult to know what triggered them.

Observed by an Ives School teacher in his "higher ability" vocational-training class, David spoke with dignity and clarity, although he was repetitive. When he said "Hello," he was friendly, although with a "touch-me-not" quality. In his work, he was careful and precise. He made sense as he talked and was clearly in touch with reality, very aware of people and his surroundings. Nevertheless, there was a lack of give-and-take in conversation, a lack of spontaneity in his social and emotional reactions, and a lack of depth in relationships with the people around him.

In the communication disorders program, David continued to improve in his ability to handle social situations. He participated in nonclass activities such as lunch, trips, athletics, and recess. David was considered the star achiever of his group. Academically, however, it was believed he had reached a plateau beyond which he probably would not go.

After graduation from the special education high school, David joined a supervised workshop at a local *community house*, where he stuffed envelopes, labeled packages, and did mail sorting and collating jobs. He worked in several community businesses, such as a dry cleaner, a printing company, and a buckle company. But the State of Connecticut, at that point, had no money for job coaches, so David was limited to his workshop and couldn't find subsidized employment elsewhere. He seemed a little less in touch, more withdrawn, than at the time of his graduation from high school two years earlier.

The following are selected quotes from the staff of the workshop which convey a picture of David as an adult:

> David socializes often with peers and staff, although he prefers staff interaction to peers. He is for the most part cooperative and will participate in program activities. . . .
> He is currently on a behavior program to increase his peer interaction. He handles conflicts by talking out loud to himself and handles his problems by asking staff for assistance. David can be bothered over the smallest thing, which can make him very upset, but he has no major disruptive behavior or problems at the present time. He has excellent hygiene and dressing skills. He has shaving skills and is aware of matching his clothes. He is aware of

neighborhood surroundings, and he walks to the store and other places in his neighborhood independently. . . .

David currently uses the community house van to travel to work. He has good table manners and is aware of cleaning up after he finishes eating. In the area of functional education, he has basic reading, writing, and math skills. He has basic knowledge of safety rules and survival skills.

David's leisure time remains a problem. He has continued to live at home while attending the supervised workshop and has little exposure to the kinds of recreation he should enjoy as a young adult. His protective family has rejected all suggestions that he live in a group home.

Growing up, David was most fortunate to have the father and mother he did. They were devoted to him and did everything they could for his well-being and development. Mr. Ellis held a good job as a machinist in a factory and was a man of determination and character. Mrs. Ellis wanted to stay home while David and his three younger brothers needed her. Both parents were young, handsome, very dignified, yet warm and friendly. David was constantly encouraged by the loving support of his father and mother and, as they got older, his brothers.

When David was at home, he kept to himself, often to such an extent that it seemed that he was "not there." He appeared to be unaware of the presence of other persons or of their conversation. Mr. Ellis tended to be firm, even stern, with David, and conveyed a sense of distress that his oldest son would never be independent, able to hold a job and support a wife and children. When David was a senior in high school, Mr. Ellis thought he might teach David to drive. He dropped this plan after the school social worker pointed out that his son did not notice physical landmarks and that, because David was socially "at sea," he was easy prey for strangers.

In the early years, the Ellises were bewildered by what was wrong with David. They recognized that he was getting excellent care at the Yale Child Study Center and trusted the people at the Ives preschool, but they still had difficulty understanding and accepting that they had a child who was different. The social worker at Ives explained that it was natural for any caring parent to feel angry, confused, and worried. When the Ellises joined a parents' group at Ives, they were able to share their feelings about David and respond to guidance about managing his behavior. They also received help from the physician at the Yale Child Study Center, especially in the area of educational guidance. At one point, David's mother repeated several times to his teacher at Ives, "Without all of you, David and we—we would have been lost."

Compared to the child who entered Ives rigid, withdrawn, and speaking only five words in a whisper, the adult David is a tribute to his intelligent, unflaggingly supportive parents, to the sensitive teachers and speech therapists who taught him from preschool through high school, and finally to the social workers, supervisors, and work coaches in his work program. Nevertheless, his maladaptive behaviors remain as noted in his testing at Yale: poor eye contact, overdependence, little social contact, trouble with concentration. His conversation sometimes seems "out of context." Improved though David is, the basic characteristics of autism remain.

In October 1987, at twenty-two, David was reevaluated at the Yale Child Study Center. The testing session included both the Wechsler Adult Intelligence Scale (WAIS-R) and the Vineland Adaptive Behavior Scales. David's father was the informant for the Vineland. David was described by the examiner as a short, stocky, twenty-two-year-old black male. His speech was stilted and halting, and he was reluctant to speak. He refused to say that he was finished with a task and persisted in giving nonverbal cues (sitting back in his chair) instead. He had appropriate eye contact during testing but unusual motor movements, pointing to his chest and stroking his legs. He muttered to himself as he worked on nonverbal items. When he used this verbal mediation, his test performance improved.

David achieved these scores:

WAIS-R
Verbal IQ: 70   Performance IQ: 69   Full Scale IQ: 69

VINELAND

Domain	Standard Score	Adaptive Level	Age Equivalent
Communication:	45	Low	9 yrs. 2 mos.
Daily Living:	57	Low	8 yrs. 11 mos.
Socialization:	49	Low	7 yrs. 4 mos
Motor skills (est.)	73	Moderately low	4 yrs. 3 mos.
Adaptive Behavior Composite:	47	Low	8 yrs. 6 mos.

ABC
78: Probably autistic

On the WAIS-R, David achieved a full-scale IQ score of 69, in the mild-deficient range of mental retardation. There was no significant difference between his verbal scale score (70) and his performance scale score (69). In view of David's enjoyment of reading history, it was interesting that he showed a relative strength (in the average range) on a task requiring the placing of pictures in a logical sequence. This test evaluates the ability to comprehend and evaluate a situation utilizing nonverbal reasoning. Anticipation, visual organization, and temporal sequencing are involved.

On the Vineland, David obtained an adaptive behavior composite score of 47. This incorporates communication, daily living skills, and socialization. This put David in the low range of normal adults in his age group. He was not stronger in one area than any other. These formal test results are congenial with other evaluations of David as having made great improvements over the years, while continuing to be impaired in aspects of intellectual and social functioning.

6 • A DESIRE TO RELATE TO OTHERS: KAREN STANLEY

born May 14, 1962

When Karen Stanley was three-and-a-half, her family pediatrician referred her to the Yale Child Study Center for developmental and psychological diagnosis. He suspected she might be autistic. Karen did not talk and seemed slow in other phases of development, such as toilet training, understanding simple instructions, and engaging in play with her age-group peers. Her physical development had been somewhat slow, and she was sensitive to sounds. The Stanleys said that Karen spoke only three words: "mine," "mama," " 'ghetti," They felt that Karen at times put a wall between herself and others. Often they were not sure whether she understood them or not, but they were beginning to suspect that she understood more than she acknowledged. The Stanleys added that Karen did not seek out other children and had no idea of cooperative play. The interview concluded with a description of the Stanleys as "a warm family."

Serial observations by the developmental pediatricians and other members of the Yale Child Study Center staff were performed to measure Karen's level of skill on developmental tests, her social relationships, and emotional development.

In the clinic's intake report, her mother described Karen as "vivacious, happy, strong-willed, persistent, likes to rock on a rocking horse, to empty drawers, spin pan lids, play in the sandpile. She seems to enjoy members of the family and loves her kitty." She was also "sweet, charming, vigorous, active, and quick," but minimally interested in toys, often quite content to be alone, not seeking affection and not speaking. Her mother found it difficult to say why Karen had seemed "fragile" and "somehow different" from birth, in spite of being physically healthy and growing normally.

In addition to her generally delayed development in motor skills, problem solving, and speech, Karen exhibited lack of interest in social interaction and social communication, absence of communicative speech, restricted patterns of behavior, pervasive anxiety, unusual preoccupation with objects and sensations, and deficits in the ability to play. Her deviant unresponsiveness and her precarious attachment to and lack of social communication with other persons were especially conspicuous. No physical or neurological abnormalities were found. After the evaluation, the specialist at Yale told Mrs. Stanley that they had diagnosed Karen as having "atypical development with autistic behavior." She then described infantile autism to Mrs. Stanley, who, at first, was shaken and bewildered.

The doctors who examined Karen believed her developmental disorder was most likely inborn, and that she would require specialized educational and other services in order to achieve her maximal development. While the long-term outlook was admittedly bleak, the doctors created an appropriate plan for handling Karen's behavior: to begin "putting her in touch with her emotions" and to find the best school for her. Karen's parents soon began to set the plan in motion.

Once the diagnosis had been made, Karen's parents were very eager to have answers to their questions and have help with her. Professor Stanley, Karen's father, was described as "soft-spoken, deliberate, dispassionate," as if he were presenting the doctors with an academic problem. His concern for Karen, nevertheless, was evident in the many questions that he asked. Mrs. Stanley, a warm, direct, and intensely vocal woman, was to prove indefatigable in her pursuit of what was best for Karen. Mrs. Stanley asked in the intake interview, "Is her development pattern serious? Or will she catch up at her own speed?" Many parents will empathize with the ambivalence and confusion this question reflects.

Mrs. Stanley, explaining Karen's condition to the rest of her family, wrote this: "Karen has no brain damage or physical impairment of any kind. Her difficulty lies in her personality structure, and it is a constitutional one. Her personality is described as atypical. Lacking the usual resources of a child, her growth and learning have been slowed. Her problems fall within the limits of what is now described as the autistic child." She concluded her letter by saying that not knowing what was wrong with Karen was far worse than knowing. She also added that whether Karen would achieve normal maturity was a great question still.

In the spring of 1966, when Karen was four, she entered the Elizabeth Ives School for Special Children. She was apprehensive about everything and clung, frightened, to her teachers for safety and reassurance. Characteristic of her behavior at the time was her compulsion to flush the toilet. She would stand by the toilet, jumping up and down, flapping her hands, hypnotized by the whirling water. Her teacher was kept busy running to the bathroom, where she would inevitably find Karen. One of Karen's strengths, however, was her apparent desire to relate to people. In this respect she differed from most of the other autistic children at Ives, and indeed, other "special" children in general.

After several months at Ives, Karen had made some academic progress, though this was quite limited. She knew the numbers from one to three but could not really use them, and she could follow simple, one-step spoken directions. She was able to recite the alphabet, although she was unable to associate the sounds of the letters with their written form. She was beginning to read and learn the basic vocabulary of a preprimer, but she had difficulty following sentences from left to right because she did not see words as a whole and therefore could not follow a word-to-word progression. (Later, at her boarding school, her teachers used cardboard frames to teach Karen to read.)

Karen had some severe visual-perception and visual-motor problems. She could not, for instance, cut with scissors (she was twenty before she could cut out a valentine), zip a zipper, or snap a snap. When she came to Ives, she could not follow a stencil with a pencil, because she could not hold the stencil with one hand and at the same time control the pencil with the other to make the outline. She could not coordinate this until the end of her second year at the preschool.

During her second year, Karen had a special teacher who took her home for the afternoons. This teacher worked with Karen on self-identity and body image. She would show Karen the body parts of a doll and compare them to Karen's own body parts until Karen acquired some awareness of her own physical makeup. The teacher also had Karen do perceptual exercises, such as crawling under a broomstick held a foot or so above the ground, to show her how her body related in size and form to other objects. Through such patient instruction, Karen developed some sense of her own size and body.

During the summer when Karen was six, she went to a private summer school for normal children, accompanied by a special teacher. There she was helped with her anxiety around other children and slowly became used to being in a group. Her general level of anxiety and apprehension also lessened, and this helped her with some of her academic tasks: She began to be able to say four- and five-word sentences and to put several sentences together. At Ives, she began consistently to stay with the children of her group, although she tended to relate to other children best through teasing them.

During the next year it became clear that Karen was ready for a more advanced program than Ives could offer, and after discussions among the people at Ives, the Stanleys, the local public school system's social worker, and the doctor at the Yale Child Study Center, the decision was made to send Karen to a private elementary school for developmentally impaired children, many of whom had emotional problems also. This proved to be inappropriate for Karen. She was overwhelmed in a class of six and unable to relate to the other children or participate in group activities. The following year she was sent to another local private school for more severely learning-disabled children and adolescents. She stayed in this school from the time she was nine until she was twelve. As Karen got older, this turned out to be a pattern: progressively she had to be placed in groups of younger and/or less able children because of her impairments.

Between ages seven and thirteen, Karen was treated by a child psychiatrist who helped her to develop and begin to use her innate capacities. This psychiatrist was able to penetrate Karen's world—her very obsessions, her interest in birds and plants—and bring out her ability to relate to people. He began, with Karen's help, by dismantling a toilet, explaining each step as he went. Karen was enthralled. His technique was to involve Karen as much as possible in the learning process, and with her participation, he expanded to bird books, recordings of bird songs, and from there to plants and insects. Karen began to acquire more self-confidence through this therapy. Soon she knew many birds' and insects' names and types of habitats, and could recognize particular birds' songs. She also learned how to look up their names in the index of her bird book, following three-digit numbers. As Karen improved, it became apparent to the therapist and her teachers that Karen had a remarkable memory.

As Karen approached adolescence, she was ready for a more structured life among her age-group peers, and so, at thirteen, she was sent to an out-of-state residential school for developmentally disabled teenagers. There she had peer companionship on a twenty-four-hour basis and was subject to peer models and pressure, which, it was hoped, could be helpful. The danger of a residential school was that Karen and the other teenagers there would become isolated—increasingly unable to interact with normal children their age. Nevertheless, apart from its limitations, the school offered a good total program of special education, peer-group living with supervision, psychotherapy, medical care, and pre-vocational training.

At first Karen responded well to the new school, but, after a time, she became anxious and unhappy and developed "negative behavior." Karen had been placed in a house with several psychotic teenage girls. This was the closest the school could come to an appropriate place for her. Because Karen was, and still is, very sensitive to loud noises, the screaming and violent behavior of her housemates was unbearable for her, and she reacted with emotional explosions and out-of-control behavior. The school's response was to put her on medication— loxitane—for the first time in her life. Instead of helping, however, the medication produced emotional withdrawal, sadness, and a subdued manner. Karen's previously happy sparkle flickered and threatened to go out. The medication was continued for one year, then stopped. In time, Karen bounced back, and although she remained subdued, she began to enjoy herself and make progress.

Karen responded particularly well to the pre-vocational program at the school, which taught self-care basics: what to wear if it was cold or hot, and what clothes generally were appropriate. These were things that "normal" children learn readily but that emotionally and developmentally disabled children have difficulty understanding the need for. Karen had to be taught to wear a petticoat underneath a sheer summer dress, to wash her hair and her face, to use a deodorant, how to understand menstruation, and how to care for herself in matters of cleanliness. She learned good personal hygiene and became quite interested in clothes and proud of keeping herself looking well. Karen's favorite courses were sewing and cooking.

Karen's basic anxiety had not been eliminated, however. She was still tense and avoided eye contact. On a psychological re-evaluation performed when she was seventeen, she tested, on average, at a second-grade, six-month level. As evidence of her perceptual and visual–motor deficits, she showed distortions and an inability to copy a whole geometric design or to stop one she had started. Her view of the world was "global": She had no ability to discriminate among the different facets of her environment. As a result, she saw her environment as generally threatening. She dealt with everything in structured, constricted, concrete, nonabstract terms. The evaluation summary concluded that Karen suffered from moderate retardation, a high anxiety level, withdrawal from personal relations, depression, low self-esteem, poor reality testing (i.e., her anxiety prevented her from seeing reality clearly), and severe visual dysfunction.

Karen's parents, teachers, and doctors concluded from these results that she would probably always need to live under supervision. But they also felt that she needed a new residential environment to help her develop some independence. A boarding school for young autistic adults and teenagers, run by a group called Pioneer, Inc., had just opened in a town near Karen's home. Karen transferred there when she was seventeen.

At the new boarding school, Karen roomed with two girls who became like sisters to her. The staff at the school worked to "reach" Karen and help her use her own capacities. Although she was afraid and timid at first, Karen slowly began to open up. Her self-confidence was encouraged by some small but significant cosmetic changes. She had her hair cut and styled in a bob she could care for on her own. She went to an orthodontist for braces, which not only straightened her teeth but improved her appearance and consequently her self-esteem. She took renewed interest in dressing attractively, matching her hair ribbons to her dress. The increased pride she had in herself improved her ability to relate to people. At times she was even playful. Once, when her teacher spilled some coffee, Karen exclaimed laughingly, "You slob!" (a peer contribution to her vocabulary). She had a boyfriend among the residents of her house, and she often said to him, "You hate me, Joe," while her eyes sparkled. She had learned increasingly to understand feelings and to express her own feelings directly. She learned how to get her boyfriend to say he loved her. To another boy who was leaving school she said, "We'll miss you, Dan." Another time she remarked, "I'm really sad. I miss my folks."

The Pioneer school ran a number of vocational training programs, among them bottle sorting (for recycling), furniture refinishing, silk-screening, and bakery work. Karen took part in bottle sorting and silk-screening T-shirts. She also worked in the bakery and as a clerk in the school's gift shop.

Karen was at ease with her family. At a lunch a teacher of hers attended, Karen helped to get the meal ready, chattering all the while to her mother. She passed the wine and crackers, and members of the family affectionately joked with her. When lunch was delayed, Karen chastised her father for holding things up by shouting, "Dad, lunch—come on! I'm starving!"

When Karen turned twenty-one, her living situation changed again, this time out of bureaucratic necessity. As with the special education programs in the public schools, funding, which was paid by the local public school system from a combination of state, federal, and local sources, stopped when a child reached twenty-one. As far as the Stanleys were concerned, in light of Karen's good functioning and improved flexibility in personal relationships, she could live at home. But at home she would have no meaningful job, no peers, no community involvement, and no tightly structured life designed to handle her deficiencies.

In Karen's residential program, there had been seventeen other young adults over twenty years of age. Since all of their parents faced the same funding problem, with the cooperation of the Pioneer school, they organized a group under the guidance of the state Department of Mental Retardation to find an answer. In Connecticut, the Department of Mental Retardation takes responsibility for placing such over-twenty-one-year-olds in living and job situations in communities. The parents felt that a supervised living situation was still clearly needed for most of their children. None of these handicapped young adults would be able to continue to progress without a carefully designed and executed program—which, of course, involved peers and skilled teachers. The parents also felt that the large, impersonal institutions, with their inadequate staffing and large number of "patients," would rob these young people of their chance for continued independence and development. Moreover, these young adults were not "patients": They were not sick; they had disabilities that could be partially overcome.

The parent group was determined to provide a residence for their children designed for training in independent living. After a year of strenuous activity, meetings, and fund raising (in which the young adults also took part), and after some of the parents had contributed personal funds, they had sufficient money for a down payment on a small apartment building and the beginnings of the new program: "Maple Avenue House." In conjunction, Pioneer, Inc. rented a store nearby to house the silk-screen shop and a gift shop. The school also had overall responsibility for the apartment building and the vocational training.

Maple Avenue House was ready when Karen was twenty-one. She lived there for four years with five other young adults and two staff as supervisors. The residents organized their own lives and did their own shopping, cooking, and housekeeping with the help of the staff. Each one had a job in the community.

Karen at first worked at silk-screening T-shirts and helping with second-hand items to be sold. Because of her attractive appearance and appealing way with people, she was to be trained as a clerk. But waiting on customers confused her, so when the bakery opened the following year, she was placed there.

At Maple Avenue House, Karen had her own studio apartment. She took her lunch to work and had dinner in the communal dining room. She took a bus to the bakery where she helped with baking bread, doughnuts, cookies, and pies. She was paid thirty-five dollars a week. She used her salary for buying jewelry and tapes of bird songs and for going out for pizza, movies, and similar group activities.

Karen still retained her pervasive anxiety, vividly illustrated by an incident which occurred during a visit to her room by one of her former teachers. Mrs. Stanley left the room briefly, carefully telling Karen that she was going to the bathroom across the hall. Although Karen knew her teacher, she was immediately uneasy, as if what kept her organized and safe had gone. She knew that her mother was nearby, yet she started pacing the floor, muttering. Told her mother would be back immediately, Karen said, "I'll go find her." She ran out of the room and down the stairs to the main floor, but had acquired enough self-control not to run out of the building.

When Karen was twenty-six, the director of Maple Avenue House met with Karen, the Stanleys, and the supervisor of the regional program to assess Karen's progress. The feeling was that Karen was ready to move to a facility where she could live a bit more independently. She had improved quite a bit in general and was more outgoing: She had even taken long bus and plane trips by herself (with the help of Traveler's Aid) to visit family members. The participants tried to create a "road map" to help others make better plans for Karen's future.

Karen showed enjoyment and intense interest in the meeting. At one point, the director asked Karen, "Who is important in your life, Karen?" She then showed Karen a drawing of a large circle containing concentric circles with Karen's name in the middle. Karen named her roommates, her cat, and her boss at the bakery readily, but she thought of naming her parents only after some prodding.

They then went on to Karen's likes and dislikes. She quickly mentioned shopping and jewelry, as well as her cat, fishing, cleaning fish but not eating them, and tapes—especially of bird songs. Karen seemed confused when asked to describe her dislikes, so her mother mentioned that Karen had always hated loud noise and confusion. She was afraid of parades, for instance. Karen spoke up at once to say, "Hate carnival rides." Her impaired depth perception was probably responsible for her fear of amusement park activities, and she still panicked at the prospect of going down a steep incline of any kind.

It was agreed that what was successful in treating Karen was "repetition and immersion." Karen has accomplished the most through constant repetition and being with someone who demonstrated and coached as she performed a task. Mrs. Stanley added that whenever Karen wanted very much to do something, eventually, through her own perseverance, she was able to do it. From early on she had sought contact and relations with other people despite her problems in doing so. As an adult, she has been motivated by pride in her achievements and by praise from someone she liked.

It was also noted that Karen's consistent weakness in living skills was the shallowness of her social contacts. She had also been unable to defend herself against taunting, teasing, or the aggressiveness of others, but in that she had improved. Her poor visual–motor skills, poor verbal intake, and limited verbal expression all continued to play a part in her difficulties.

Karen was rated by her vocational counselor as about fifty percent independent and responsible in general. She initiated and carried out getting a haircut, which involved using the telephone, although dialing was difficult for her. She took good care of her cat, using a chart of chores to be performed. Her grooming and personal care were good, and she took her vitamin C without having to be reminded. At the bakery, however, her poor concentration and visual–motor ineptness, and her inability to take sequential instructions, made it hard for her to learn new skills. In spite of some improvement, it was clear that the bakery was the wrong placement. Karen would always need a job coach, but her advisors agreed that she might be able to share an apartment with another disabled young adult since she has conquered each preceding step of development.

As a result of this meeting, Karen transferred to Algonquin House, a supervised three-bedroom house also administered by Pioneer, where she now lives with two other developmentally disabled women. A crisis ensued several months after Karen moved there. Because of funding problems, Algonquin House was threatened with closing. The crisis was averted, but the bakery where Karen worked had to be sold. She and her workmates were moved to the regional vocational center, where they now cook and serve lunch.

Karen participates in trips to places such as national parks, sponsored by Pioneer. She is able, with a supervisor, to go to a supermarket and shop from a grocery list successfully. She still can't make change, however, so the clerk must take the money and count it out for her.

Karen has made almost miraculous progress from the delicate, vulnerable four-year-old who arrived at the Ives School. Her

perceptual handicaps have been modified through patient training, although they continue to limit her behavior and personality. It took her many months, at the age of twenty-two, to learn
how to flute a pie crust. She managed to ride an escalator
independently for the first time when she was twenty-five. And
while she is more in touch now with the people around her
than at any time before, there are still times when she seems lost,
remote, and tense, gripped by an anxiety she cannot control.

As an adult, Karen still does not talk spontaneously most of the
time, and she avoids eye contact. Her speech, though often
clear, is nevertheless staccato and limited in vocabulary and
phraseology. When she is tired of a conversation, she will turn
away as if the other person were not there. Karen still has
compulsive gestures, and occasionally, when she is talking, she
covers her face with her hands in a sudden convulsive movement of her body. Yet, in general, her relationship to others has
improved. She will even, if asked, offer her cheek for a kiss,
which is quite unusual, as autistics are generally uncomfortable
with such intimate contact.

    In the October 1987 testing at the Yale Child Study Center,
she achieved the following scores:

WAIS-R
Verbal IQ: 62   Performance IQ: 52   Full Scale IQ: 55

Vineland

Domain	Standard Score	Adaptive Level	Age Equivalent
Communication:	20	Low	4 yrs. 3 mos.
Daily Living:	49	Low	7 yrs. 9 mos.
Socialization:	44	Low	5 yrs. 9 mos.
Adaptive Behavior Composite:	27	Low	5 yrs. 11 mos.

ABC
126: Autistic

As measured by the Wechsler Adult Intelligence Scale-Revised (WAIS-R), Karen placed in the moderately retarded range of intellectual functioning. Her verbal, performance, and full-scale IQ scores were all consistent with one another. It was striking to note, however, that Karen earned one of her highest scores on similarities, a test of verbal abstract reasoning. Such relative skill in an individual with limited overall cognitive capability is rather uncommon. It suggests that she may have the capacity for some degree of conceptual, reflective reasoning.

On the basis of an interview with Karen's mother, using the Vineland survey form, Karen obtained an adaptive behavior composite score of 27, which places her in the low range when compared to all adults in her peer group.

The psychologist described Karen as a slightly overweight young woman with dark hair, heavy eyebrows, and a fair complexion. She was dressed casually in bright, stylish clothing. She was friendly and cooperative throughout the assessment. She volunteered that she was soon going to have her ears pierced and that her brother was going to be married, and she seemed quite happy about both events. Karen tried hard on all assessment tasks. However, when unsure of an answer, she would not attempt to guess.

"I had to identify her emotions for her . . ."
by Elizabeth Stanley

Diagnosis and Prognosis

In early 1966, after several months of careful examination and study, the Yale Child Study Center told me that my three-year-old child was different—"atypical" was the word they used. They went on to say that her atypicalness fell within the broad syndrome known as "autism." I had never heard the term. They told me that she was born with built-in deficits, with no cause yet known. It was simply the way she was constitutionally constructed. This basic personality, along with its limitations, would be hers always. We had to accept and live with that.

I was terrified—at first by the cloud of mystery, and then by my gradual awakening to what it really meant, which was worse. Karen, this lovely baby we had so wanted, who was adored by all of us, including our other four children and relatives, would never be normal. Since then there has been no significant disagreement among the different specialists we have consulted on Karen's diagnosis and prognosis. All observed that Karen was not capable of imaginative play; she was withdrawn and unable to relate normally to other children. She was obsessive and perseverative. She was autistic.

By the time Karen was diagnosed, I had already known for some time that there was something wrong with her. When she was two, we and our five children lived for a year in a large city in the Orient. Before we left the U.S., when getting the necessary immunizations at the pediatrician's office, I hesitantly raised my hidden fears about Karen. Although none of her development was out of step with what I knew to be normal, she seemed slow: She wasn't speaking; she felt limp; she lacked ordinary aggression (my other children at her age would have been all over the doctor's office, climbing on chairs, or pulling papers from his desk). I said she seemed docile, too quiet. Was something wrong? The pediatrician mulled that over a bit, gazed thoughtfully at Karen, then reassured me: All children develop at different rates and over different spans of time; she was within normal bounds.

Our voyage abroad by freighter was a lively experience: two months at sea, visiting many ports in the Mediterranean, the Red Sea, the Middle East, and India. But I grew more troubled about Karen. Although I took two trunks full of toys, games, and books for the children, she touched none of them. She would not play with any of us, although she enjoyed it when we tossed her about and tickled her. The only amusement she found was splashing in the sink or bathtub in our room, and being carried about by the crewmen, who adored children.

After our arrival in the East, following the custom there, I employed an aide to take care of Karen. I also enrolled her in a small nursery group. But while all the others joined in play, or listened to stories, or sang songs, Karen sat on the fringe poking at the sand at her feet. She stood all alone, isolated.

After a while, we started to refer to Karen as "the quiet one." We began to feel increasingly cut off, even rejected, by her. At her age, after all, children look at you, hear you, laugh at and with you, annoy you. Not Karen. I suspected that she needed medical help, and, so far from home, I became increasingly worried and at times nearly frantic.

When we returned, in the fall of 1965, I immediately took Karen to the Yale Child Study Center, to undergo professional scrutiny. While we awaited the outcome, friends and family tried to reassure us. But in those assurances I dimly sensed their need to protect me from some horrible truth they themselves had begun to fear. "After all," they reasoned, "what do you expect? All of you dote on her and baby her to death. She doesn't have to talk or do anything. Before long she'll get tired of that, and then you will see a big change. Einstein, you know, didn't talk until he was three." We needed to believe them, so we did.

Meanwhile, we enrolled her in a nursery school, and our experience there prepared us for the reality the extensive testing would soon reveal. The teacher was completely baffled by Karen, so much so that she began to question her own competence. Finally, she insisted Karen must be deaf. Worse, she worried that Karen didn't like her and therefore would not respond to her as the others did. She felt hurt, a failure. I felt the same.

After three months of careful examination, observation, and consultation by the staff of the Child Development Clinic at the Yale Child Study Center, our doctor there told us the tragic truth. Karen was not deaf; she could hear a pin drop. This developmental specialist, her eyes full of a dread her professionalism could not hide, said Karen suffered from autism, an affliction for which there was no known cure. Education was the only possible therapy.

The problem was that deficits in the formation of Karen's personality were interfering with its normal development. Karen had no sense of her own identity, and she could not locate and use her own emotions. "You must get through to her, press yourself upon her, barrage her, make her hear you and respond. We are certain she can. You must reach her." I could not miss the desperate insistence in the doctor's voice.

The doctor went on. She said there was one other thing I had to do: I had to identify Karen's emotions for her, and then interpret them for her and teach her what they were and the appropriate responses to them. I had no idea what this meant. For a long time Karen had seemed incapable of feeling or expressing any emotion. Now the doctor was telling me that she really had emotions but could not understand what they were for or how to express them. Likewise, the doctor said that

Karen had intelligence but could not use it. She could not relate normally to people or even to her physical surroundings.

As I listened, my mind whirled and my throat went dry. It all seemed unreal. I realized Karen's responses and behavior were distressingly impersonal and sometimes bizarre. Now I was told I had to develop some way to force her to do what she apparently could not do on her own—hear me, respond to me, deal with me, act like a human being. My God, what was she? Even dogs lick your hands, jump on you, invite you to play. Was she a sub-being of some sort? Could she ever learn, respond naturally? What if she couldn't? Would she become a vegetable and have to be "put away"? There are no words to describe those moments, the pain and terror I felt as I walked out of that office.

On arriving home, I opened the door. Full of apprehension, I went to the kitchen and put my purse on the table. Karen stood in the hallway. She acted as if I were not there. I looked at her. She did not look at me; I wasn't "there." "Karen," I called softly, "come here." She did not move. "Karen," I said, louder. She looked at the floor. "Karen!" I shouted. She did not move. Tears of desperation filled my eyes. With both hands, I picked up a fat cookbook, lifted it over my head, and slammed it with all my might on the table, sending the salt and pepper shakers flying. "Karen!" I screamed. She turned and looked at me. She heard! I had reached her! She could respond! I was stunned. I knelt before her, gathered her in my arms, and sobbed. This was where I had to begin. What to do? Who would help? What would happen to her, to all of us, to me? Karen said, did nothing.

So began the long trek to today.

Karen and Our Family

At the very time in the life of a child when one expects the beginning of social interaction, Karen withdrew from us. She was rigid in body, fragile in bearing, vulnerable, and very frightened. All stimuli confused her unbearably and caused her either to recede or to engage in what we thought of as bizarre behavior. She seemed to be deaf. She found refuge in the bathroom, where she flushed the toilet endlessly; or she sat on the floor and rubbed the feet of a bronze statue we had brought with us from the East.

She immersed herself in things, in objects, in meaningless behavior. She was withdrawn, out of touch. Her gaze fixated at times on certain objects, such as the reflector pan of the stove or a crack in the table top. She screamed in terror when we blew up a balloon. She poked things repeatedly that caught her glance: a piece of jewelry on another person's dress or a mole on the neck of a friend.

And the greatest problem of all for her future was her very poor reasoning ability and severe thought disorder. She had little to no ability for abstract thinking: She learned by rote, retaining what she held in her unusual memory. Pain, sorrow, anger—all these were beyond her. Such concepts as under, over, near, and far were like a foreign language to her, to be learned and routinely applied.

Her speaking as it emerged was often unrelated to anything and made little sense to others. She repeated a word or phrase over and over. As she learned speech, it was echolalic— automatically repeating what another person had just said.

She had no idea of spatial relationships, of similarities, differences, or opposites. She had little sense of her own body or of her body's relationship to the space around it. She seemed not to know that she had arms and legs, ears and eyes, or what they were for.

She insisted on objectifying anything (including living things) so she could touch it, handle it, mouth the words for it endlessly. She treated animate things as inanimate and inanimate things as animate. She turned people into things to be poked. She would pat and stroke a desk, or put a barn-door hook-and-eye latch in the baby buggy and push it about. Records were for spinning, not for listening. Dolls were for pulling apart. She even tried repeatedly to pull off her own head or stick it in the toilet.

She was tense and fearful. When frustrated, she would hit herself, pull up her skirt, or recede into a corner, thumb in mouth. She dug at her fingers until they bled.

In all, this one fact stood out: She could not relate to people as people. Locked inside this vacant isolation, she was virtually unreachable by anyone, beginning with her family, and of course I feared she could eventually back out of human contact entirely and into a world none of us would be able to enter. The prospects were horrifying.

Worst of all, she did not know us, who we were, or that she was our baby girl and our other children's sister. She had no idea who she was, that she was a girl, a daughter, a sister, a playmate, a person. She did not play with her siblings or delight them as babies always do. This was, I felt, a loss for my other children beyond speaking. Likewise, she did not know me as her mother: I had no special meaning for her. She could easily walk off with the next stranger on the street, and sometimes did. She didn't know the difference. It was years before she knew who her parents and siblings were, and where and what home and family were. All of us felt rejected.

I was nearly crushed. If you can penetrate the heart of a mother and perceive what really feeds her inner being and makes her enjoy being a mother, it surely includes the wonder and excitement and ineffable satisfaction of the response of her child to her. But this could not be; it was impossible to mother Karen. I was screened out. I had no cue from her to go on; I was at a dead end. I could only do things for her or to her and see that she was fed and clothed. The distance between such care and mothering is vast.

In those early days I could only think that I, in some way
unknown to me, had caused her problem. I am sure every
mother of an autistic person suffers this torture. But in time I
came to understand that the cause lay in Karen's own constitutional makeup and her consequent development. Slowly, I
began to realize that these symptoms of autism were not
rejection of me or of us but rather her escape from impossible-
to-endure confusion and inner turmoil over which she had no
other control. The symptoms were, in fact, her very means of
survival. We would have to find out how to get around or
through them to her to help her take control and release the
real person within.

Parents and Family at Risk

The difficulties an autistic person brings to a family are enor-
mous, especially for the mother. You go on being a wife, a
mother to the others, a neighbor, a friend, a relative—taking up
those relationships while you try not to allow the autistic
person to absorb you to the detriment of your life. You try to
avoid feeling guilty, for if the mother feels guilty, the problem
is only compounded. And no matter how much you give, the
autistic person still needs more.

Siblings often feel abandoned by a mother given over to
the care of an autistic child. They feel neglected or, worse, they
feel guilty that their demands might increase their mother's
already too-great burden. It is easy for them to fear that adding
to their mother's worries might push her over the brink. They
do not feel free to express what might be ordinary discontent
about their situation.

In such circumstances, how can a normal adolescent work
through the ambivalence and the complexities of growing up?
This was especially true in the 1960s and 1970s, when Karen
was young, which was a time of great social upheaval and

disenchantment of the young with the establishment of which we, the parents, were of course a part. So Karen's siblings became mute and tended to go their own ways, missing sorely what they needed from their parents.

Their apparent alienation made things difficult for me, too. Because they were normal, I expected them to do a lot for themselves and to help with Karen. It was very easy for me to feel everyone left me with the burden, isolated and alone. Such feelings on my part only increased their worries and drove them further away. And the problem worsened.

My husband was usually not directly involved in the day-to-day care of Karen. Some men, my husband included, find the pain of having and caring for an autistic child simply too great to live with intimately and still carry on their work. I now see that it might have destroyed him, as he feared it would me. He had to protect himself, and this meant distancing himself as he could from the ever-present trouble.

My husband did help where he could—with the transportation of the children to their social and school obligations and of Karen to her numerous appointments and programs. He did keep steadily at his job and its demands and supported the family. He sometimes made it possible for us to get away alone where we could restore ourselves and be refreshed. He involved himself in every decision. Although relating to Karen baffled him, he cared about her and in one way or another built a strong relationship with her that today serves her well. Now he delights in her accomplishments, growth, and presence, and participates in the new challenges we face with her. He often picks her up at her residence to take her shopping and to dinner at a restaurant, a treat she always accepts with much pleasure.

Once, speaking to a parents' group, my husband said he often felt as though we were in a lifeboat. Karen had fallen overboard, and I was about to jump in after her, even though I didn't know how to swim. His job, he said, was to steady the boat and keep me from jumping. (It is the mother, after all, who jumps. How could I possibly sit there and watch my child drown?) He once told me flatly, "If it is a choice between you and Karen, I choose you." Well, in a way I was reassured and in a way threatened. What did choosing me mean? Giving up Karen? I had to keep myself and Karen stable so that such a choice would not be necessary. So I kept quiet.

And in that is the essence of the deepest isolation of all the mother of an autistic child feels. I couldn't imagine giving up Karen, yet I couldn't express to my husband or children what I was feeling, for I knew it hurt them and drove them away from me. So I increasingly felt alone, trapped. I have since learned that most mothers of autistic children do.

Karen's Education

At the time Karen was diagnosed, there was only one small school in our area that was trying to deal with autistic children: the Elizabeth Ives School for Special Children. The doctors at the Yale Child Study Center suggested we enroll her there, which we did.

In all, Karen has gone to five schools, some of them new and experimental. Three were local day schools, two were residential. From her earliest years, schooling for Karen followed a consistent pattern. She had a succession of wonderful teachers who were committed deeply to her, and who believed she could be made to hear them and to learn. Many of them believed firmly that she had a concealed intelligence and emotional sensitivity, which they sought desperately to reach and to activate. These forceful and persistent people provided Karen with the necessary structure and support for her to begin to participate in life, to respond, to speak, to know herself and let herself be known.

Fundamental to the method used was the drive to get

reaction from her. They, the teachers, and we, the parents, *demanded* a relationship with Karen, and in demanding it from her, we began to get it. She *had* to look into our eyes, hear us, and respond to us. We *insisted*. It was a gut job, not a paper exercise. It made us sweat. Teaching her reading, writing, and arithmetic at that stage seemed less relevant than nurturing a relationship in which we helped her to identify pain, anger, affection, humor, hurt, and grief and express them appropriately.

Karen's education and training went on at school and at home. Her disabilities forced us to teach her survival skills—what she had to know and do to adapt to a world she could not understand. We demanded, so far as we could, acceptable behavior. She gradually learned to look after her personal care, to take her own shower, to tidy her room, to understand and manage menstruation, to dress nicely, to greet people. Each acquired skill prepared her to learn the next, and to grow in the art of being human.

There was an additional, extremely potent, force at work for Karen. It lay within her. She *wanted* to relate to us. She *wanted* to learn and be independent. All the while she was growing up, she had not been really so out of touch as her withdrawal had made it seem. As time and schooling went on, the layers of resistance and withdrawal peeled away, and we learned that she wanted to laugh, to sing, to dance, to be with us, to draw, to pile up blocks and knock them down, to swim, to walk, to listen to records, to watch the birds, to learn the names of flowers and trees, to go places and do things.

Speech came awkwardly. At first it was hollow and regimented, then slowly her own speech emerged, clear and crisp. She learned to assert herself and defend her possessions and her privacy. She wanted friends. As she learned to express her pleasure in people she began to elicit the affection of those with whom she came in contact. Her smile took over and the pleasant person she is emerged. For all her stilted speech, she won interest and affection, and more and more people made their adjustments to her difficulties and peculiarities and related to her. They not only made her happy, they helped her to learn to live. It all came with glacial slowness. It was only after long spans of time had passed between what she had been and what she was becoming that we knew progress was being made.

As Karen learned to relate to people, her ability to learn the fundamentals of the simplest survival skills and elementary academics improved, and her inner disturbance began to give way bit by bit to inner calm. She began to take control of herself and emerge as a person. She learned more and more of the social skills that are essential to normal living. In time, we found she could not progress very much academically. We had to learn when to stop our pressure.

Over the years, Karen has been examined, evaluated, and treated by competent psychologists, psychiatrists, social workers, and educators. We have employed helpers and teachers privately. Connecticut during these years was in the forefront in taking governmental responsibility for the education of all children, even those as deeply impaired as Karen. So, happily for us, the state bore part of the horrendous cost of educating and treating her.

Adulthood and Supported Independence

After many years living at home and in group homes, Karen now lives with two other developmentally impaired women in a semi-supervised apartment in a nearby city. The state Department of Mental Retardation provides twenty hours a week of staff supervision for this semi-independent living program. In Karen's case, the staff person is a capable adult who helps Karen and her apartment mates organize their home, provide food and necessary supplies, schedule medical visits, and plan and take part in social and recreational activities. A vocational counselor helps locate jobs in the community. Thus, Karen is more and more thrown on her own resources, and often she is able to develop her own skills to meet her emerging needs. However, she still needs much help—the most difficult sort to provide—in taking responsibility for herself, and in planning and executing the means of satisfying her needs.

Given her basic deficits and the long-term care by staff persons, her progress toward increasing independence is slow. She still has no concept of numbers or money, and quite confidently empties her wallet in front of store clerks, who are then expected to take only what is needed. So far, her trust has not been betrayed. But this illustrates how much we, who parent such autistic people, must trust the fragile and often dangerous society into which we launch our children, hoping not only that they can manage, but that others will give them a hand and not harm them. With Karen, our trust has been rewarded, but I can never give up fearing for her. Even crossing the street is a major hazard because, with cars coming, she will start across the street, all the while assuring me she has "looked" and, having looked, is free to go. Looking, assessing what she sees, and transferring that into appropriate action is still a very complicated process. For Karen learns not so much by instruction as by immersion. I was never one to throw a child into a swimming pool and say "swim," but now I do it all the time with Karen. There is no alternative if she is to be able to live in the world as it is. For that goal I am willing to risk her life, to take the chance that she will make it. This is not a testimony to rashness but to my desperation and her need.

Any program in semi-independent living for an autistic person is full of risk and uncertainty. Karen is frequently on her own, busying herself at her home, traveling over the one bus route she knows to a mall which, I have learned, is like a village green, opening to her the world of shops and the possibility of meeting a friend. She takes up formerly impossible tasks such as getting herself bathed, dressed, and outside ready to meet a van that takes her to work each morning. Even managing not to lose her house key and actually being abe to put it in the lock, turn it, and open the door without a helper in sight is a major step ahead, and a building block upon which she develops more confidence and other skills. The two people who share her apartment are good friends, and they all help each other in many ways. Their apartment has become a kind of informal gathering place for others in nearby semi-independent programs. They celebrate birthdays, go out together to special events, send out for pizza, and watch TV and videos. They hang out.

Efforts are made to help Karen and her friends explore and use resources in the community, such as churches, YMCAs, health centers, libraries, movies, concerts, and eating places. Like most adults, they move about in a circle they come to know and can handle on their own. Up until two years ago, Karen lived in group homes under twenty-four-hour supervision and had never been left alone one day in her life, even at home. Until she was thirty, her entire life was programmed, supervised, and carried out under close staff supervision. She could not use a telephone or take a bus or taxi. She could not prepare her own meals, organize her daily life, plan and carry out what she wanted to do, or pay her own bills.

Now she can use the phone and, most of the time, dial it correctly. She helps clean the house and does her own laundry. She can open canned food and microwave TV dinners. She is often alone in her apartment, even for an entire weekend, sometimes preferring that to coming home to her parents. She can take the bus on a limited basis; she can call a taxi when needed. She can walk alone down her street a couple of blocks to a variety store to buy milk and bread. On Sundays she takes a taxi to church (having telephoned the previous day to arrange to be picked up). She goes to work each morning, still in a semi-supervised job, but increasingly on her own.

Karen still has major deficiencies that would confound any normal person. She cannot handle the phone reliably: She will frequently pick up the receiver and not say anything, expecting it to talk to her. She does not get messages straight. She cannot read or write beyond primitive levels. She is lost if a well-defined route is interrupted. She still does not approach others to ask for help or directions. Her recreational outlets are few, her friends limited to those at least as limited and impaired as she is. When frustrated, she may "act out" by screaming and breaking things, not yet knowing how to express her feelings appropriately and work out her frustrations in a more useful way.

As inadequate as it sometimes seems, I know Karen's life depends on the resources the state can give her in living independently and learning to manage her own life. Although I cannot see very far down the road, I am sure she can grow more and more into a life she can manage on her own. Increasingly, she will become independent, a goal once so far beyond the realm of possibility I never in my wildest dreams imagined it could happen. Well, it hasn't yet, and every week is fraught with problems. But we muddle through, and in the end, I am sure Karen will survive as her own person in her own life.

7 • UNPREDICTABLE AND TURBULENT: JOHN STARK
born June 20, 1961

When John was first at Ives, visitors, misled by his normal appearance, would often ask, "Why is that child here?" Now, as an adult, he retains a quick flashing smile and a responsive sparkle in his eyes and has an outgoing manner and appearance. He is overweight and has lost the perfect complexion and appealing features of early childhood, but people are still mystified when told of his disability. They ask, "Isn't this young man perfectly normal?" But he isn't.

John was a very difficult baby—fussy, high-strung, and crying almost continuously. He was hard to comfort although at times he quieted when held and rocked. As he grew older he had sleep problems. He was late in sitting and did not walk until he was sixteen months old. Between one and three, he often reacted with extreme fear to a variety of noises and changes in his usual environment. At other times and after the age of two-and-a-half, he often appeared jovial, very likable, with spells that the physician at the Yale Child Study Center described as "ornery." John was undiscriminating about people. Anyone could care for him as long as they gave him undivided attention. He attended a normal nursery school when he was three but got into difficulty because of his hyperactivity and impulsiveness. He was very demanding when his mother was present, and insisted that she be involved in all his activities.

His mother had become increasingly upset with John's

146

behavior and said that most of the time she was screaming at him and in tears. She often reached the saturation point. Both sets of grandparents were critical of him and of her handling of him.

John was evaluated at the Yale Child Study Center twice, the first time when he was almost three and again about a year later. The developmental evaluations at age four described him as generally awkward in motor development, with difficulties in hand skills and hand–eye coordination. His performance on nonverbal problem-solving tasks ranged between thirty and forty-two months, substantially below his age level. He became easily disoriented and overexcited or distracted, and his attention span was short. His social relationships were superficial, and his affect was bland, as though there were an emptiness within.

John used toys appropriately, but his play was fragmented, and he flitted from one activity to another. His speech production and comprehension were within normal limits. He enjoyed stories and knew many nursery rhymes. He seemed to want to be with other children but became overexcited and disoriented when with more than two others. He reacted intensely and with panic to certain noises and situations.

John was diagnosed as a neurologically impaired, emotionally disturbed child. Yale recommended psychiatric treatment for him after his second evaluation, but his parents were not ready for that. (Later he would have a period of psychotherapy.)

John entered Ives School at the age of four years and three months. He was a short, well-built child with a pink-cheeked, round face, large blue eyes, and a beguiling smile. During his first week, he was agreeable and anxiously conforming. That disintegrated rapidly into hyperactive, angry, often hysterical behavior.

John required the total attention of his teachers. His

favorite place to play was the doll corner, and with constant teacher attention and praise he could play with a toy for one or two minutes. He could not tolerate a lapse in teacher presence, and he reacted hysterically to efforts to introduce another activity or include another child in his play.

During John's first year he improved, despite absences caused by a broken leg and eye surgery to correct strabismus (a disorder where the eyes cannot both be focused at the same time). He came to realize that largely because of his verbal skills, he could do easy academic tasks better than his classmates, and this gave him self-confidence. Gradually, though still distractible and anxious, he learned to stick to an activity for a short while, and he pushed and shoved far less. He was obsessed by domestic play, such as pushing the vacuum cleaner and pretending to cook, and he spent a lot of time in water play. He also began to play, albeit superficially, with other children. Even with his progress, however, teaching John remained a daring enterprise. Despite his verbal ability, there seemed to be an intangible wall between him and everyone around him.

After three years at Ives, John was transferred to a private day school for handicapped children and adolescents, where he remained for eight years, to age fifteen. While there, he made painfully slow progress in academic areas such as math, written English, and the sciences; did modestly well in reading; and improved his motor skills through athletics. He did well in music and at school assemblies, where he distinguished himself as a master of ceremonies, ad-libbing humorously. He seemed happiest when entertaining a group and blossomed with this success. Oral reading, music, singing, and acting were his strengths. He remained severely handicapped by his emotional explosiveness.

During most summers between ages seven and fifteen, John went to a residential camp. His ability to relate to his peers improved but nevertheless remained "insubstantial," according to camp reports.

One problem John had was that his family had unrealistic expectations of him. Mr. and Mrs. Stark were both achievers: She was an accountant, and he was a teacher in a public school. The atmosphere at home was often chaotic. John was unpredictable emotionally, and could dissolve without warning into hysterical crying or shouting. Life at home was a "constant screaming match." Because John was so verbal and had such a "normal" appearance, his parents had difficulty accepting the fact that he was genuinely and permanently functionally disabled.

At fifteen, John went to a residential school for emotionally disturbed adolescents. This relieved the stress in the Stark home a bit, and John's parents thought it would help his socialization. Again, however, his improvement was minimal.

When John was seventeen, he returned home to enter a new special education program set up by the state, offering small academic classes and vocational training. He did fairly well during his four years in this setting. He was the star speller of his class, did well in reading and in English, and learned how to use a typewriter and a calculator. He remained unpredictable emotionally, however, and at the end of his first year he started group therapy. Significantly, in this group he could interpret his classmates' feelings but not his own. He could tell other members of the group how they were feeling, but he could never describe how he felt.

John started pre-vocational training his third year, working as kitchen help in a fast-food restaurant, and he did well. His employer was interested in developmentally disabled adults and gave John support and direction. In his second placement, in another fast-food restaurant, John did less well; the second employer had little understanding of his handicaps.

During his high-school summers, John went to a camp

where he worked as an aide, and through this camp he participated in track and the long jump at the Special Olympics.

In his final years at school he worked four days a week
doing more food preparation and less clean-up. He was paid
hourly for the first time.

After graduation, John worked in a downtown cafeteria
(he had long since learned to ride the bus) and then as a
volunteer janitor in the public schools. He was discouraged not
to be earning money, but his biggest heartache was his social
isolation. Since for many years his family had regarded him as
fairly capable, they felt that he did not belong in the social
programs sponsored by the Association for Retarded Adults.
John had had only casual friends at school, and none in his
neighborhood. Fortunately, he was in a special catechism class
at his local church and in a special Boy Scout troop. Still, John
had little else to do.

Then things improved. Four friends from high school
began to call him; this happened so often that John's father
gave John his own telephone. He began spending the night at
friends' houses and, in turn, had a friend stay with him. He also
developed enough self-reliance to spend long weekends alone at
home when his parents went on vacation. John grew in self-
confidence from this increased independence.

At this time, a test given John by a vocational psychologist
showed him to have impaired sensory function. He was able to
discriminate items by shape with only fifty-percent accuracy.
Discrimination of objects by size, texture, and configuration
was quite difficult for him. This limitation narrowed the range
and kind of work he could perform. For the first time, his
family accepted the fact that he was functionally retarded.
His parents had him evaluated by the Department of Mental
Retardation's local regional center, which suggested that John
apply to a special-needs school for young adults.

Thus, at the age of twenty-three, John was in a school that

featured dormitory-type living, where he shared quarters with three other developmentally disabled young men. They were all expected to have jobs, keep the apartment clean, buy food and cook meals, and participate in recreational activities. Although he did comparatively well in daily living skills and in his job as an aide in a nursing home, John frequently refused to join in group activities because of his emotional passivity, although he would go out for pizza or to a movie with others. He was more interested in activities within the apartment and in solo activities, such as music. At times he had difficulty adhering to the structure of the program, and he had not done well in vocational tests administered by the State Department of Vocational Rehabilitation (DVR).

There was a turn for the better, according to John's father, when, after repeated parental requests, the DVR agreed to re-test John. The results showed great improvement, and he was permitted to enter training in the DVR fast-foods program. John increased his participation in group activities and subsequently graduated from the school.

John now shares a condominium with another graduate of the school. They take care of all their own needs: They shop, cook, clean, and in general maintain their own apartment. The condominium is located in a convenient area of the city, where John is able to maintain contact with the other hundred or so graduates of the school. The school provides a living-skills counselor who comes in once or twice a month to help John reconcile his finances and help with any personal problems he may have. He rarely needs more assistance, however.

A job coach is still essential as a support for John at his work: With someone in control, he feels safe. He can still disintegrate emotionally when he is too excited or when he is under certain unpredictable pressures, such as the need to make quick decisions or be flexible about a change of in routine. But now he is far less likely to break down than in earlier years.

For someone who was unable to describe his feelings, John now seems to have a good perspective on himself. He describes himself as "not so moody as I used to be. I've noticed that in myself. I've just been figuring that out in my head. I *hate* going to pieces. When it happens, I say to myself: Where did I ever go wrong? Why was it always me? But now I can begin to sort out my feelings. I can open out more after one of these storms, and I do apologize to everyone." John is aware of how far he has come. "I am proud of myself," he says.

In the October 1987 testing, done when he was twenty-six, John's scores were as follows:

WAIS-R
Verbal IQ: 73   Performance IQ: 65   Full Scale IQ: 68

VINELAND

Domain	Standard Score	Adaptive Level	Age Equivalent
Communication:	65	Low	11 yrs. 3 mos.
Daily Living:	119	Moderately high	18 yrs. 11 mos.
Socialization:	111	Adequate	18 yrs. 11 mos.
Adaptive Behavior Composite:	92	Adequate	18 yrs. 11 mos.

ABC
52: Possibly autistic

The supervising psychologist's report reads as follows:

Behavioral Observations

John Stark . . . cooperated fully with all aspects of this evaluation and appeared to give his best effort. He appeared extremely proud and smiled a great deal following responses he perceived to be successes. Throughout the testing session, he made appropriate eye contact and he initiated several conversations. For example, he spontaneously described his job at a pizza restaurant. On the way to the testing room and returning, John appeared very unsure of himself in terms of his orientation in physical space. He appeared unsteady in a hall that has a slight incline followed by a slight decline and he raised his foot very high to move over a colored area rug.

Summary of WAIS-R and Vineland Interview Data

John's level of cognitive functioning was assessed with the Wechsler Adult Intelligence Scale-Revised (WAIS-R). On the WAIS-R, John achieved a Full Scale IQ score of 68, which places his performance in the Mild Deficit range of mental retardation. . . .

On the basis of an interview with John's father using the Vineland survey form, John obtained an Adaptive Behavior Composite score of 92 . . . plac[ing] his adaptive functioning in the average range and corresponds to the forty-second percentile when compared with all adults in his peer group. John had significant strengths in daily living skills and socialization. . . .

"Never take 'no' for an answer . . ."
by Carole and John Stark

We have always had a lot of confidence in John and have always wanted the best for him. Maybe it was that we saw through the surface; we felt that he had potential and could succeed despite his autism. We hoped to work through his limitations and help him succeed. We were dedicated to the idea that John would continue with his education and take advantage of all of the opportunities he could, pursuing whatever he could to find out just what it was he could and couldn't do. As a result we have often had to fight state agencies who felt that, according to their test results, he wasn't up to "par" for the competitive world.

It is John himself who has given us the confidence we have in him. He has always conveyed his ability to maintain a semblance of normality and to live in the community. While John was growing up, however, it seemed that every school he went to was only giving him about half the kind of education he needed, and he did not progress as we felt he could. Finally, when he was twenty-one, we found the right school for him, one where they had the living skills program—job skills and so on—to give him the necessary background to be in the competitive world and able to live on his own with a roommate. He has handled everything very well.

We have always had difficulty with the administrative agencies and their attitude toward John and his capabilities. It seemed they were always saying he couldn't do something, while we thought he could. At the last school John attended, one of the requirements for graduation was that the student work at paid employment for a period of six months. The school worked in conjunction with the Connecticut Department of Mental Retardation (DMR), which dealt with handicapped individuals. The DMR did vocational skills testing to find where each student's job skills were strongest. After John was tested, they felt he would be best suited for general maintenance work, i.e., mowing, raking, and general cleaning. He was sent to several various job sites and his performance was evaluated.

The evaluation proved to be poor. John was found to be lethargic, lacked interest in his work, and didn't seem to have the physical stamina for that type of job. The DMR decided that John was not suitable for competitive employment in the community. We were outraged. They had ignored John's experience, acquired before he entered this school, of working for a cleaning service for several months and, for many years before that, working for a local restaurant as a dishwasher and food preparation person. The DMR recommended that John wait for placement at a sheltered workshop, and advised a thorough physical examination, although their own physical examination had not revealed any health problems.

While he waited for placement, John worked at a variety of volunteer jobs. One was at a home for the aged, where he worked as a transporter, taking patients to physical therapy and returning them to their rooms when their therapy was over. He did this well, but every now and again he became a bit bossy and had to be reprimanded gently. He would also enter uninvited into conversations, and while patients enjoyed his friendly nature, the staff was sometimes a bit put out. The staff would correct John when his behavior was out of line, and he stayed on that job for several months.

By then it was time for another planning and placement team (PPT) meeting at his school. The PPT was a group of professionals, composed of a school psychologist, teacher, vocational teacher, the program director, and parents, who met to help plan the balance of John's academic and social-skills program and, most important, to decide in what area he could earn a living. After much discussion, we decided to ask the

DMR to retest John's vocational skills; this time in the area of food services. The reason was that John had shown many changes in attitude and ability since his previous tests.

We heard from the DMR very soon after the PPT meeting. They informed us that John's name had come to the top of their list for placement in a sheltered workshop. We told the DMR about the recent PPT decision and emphasized that his improvement over the past year was the basis for our desire to have him tested again. The DMR insisted that it was highly unlikely that anyone, in such a short period, could have made an improvement significant enough to warrant a retest. They said that they had discussed it with the school and that they all—DMR *and* PPT staff—felt that John should take this slot at the sheltered workshop or he might not get another chance. The DMR also strongly implied that if John did not, his file might be closed. This would mean that John might not be able to use any DMR services in the future. We felt a good deal of pressure, even threat, in what the DMR said to us.

As parents, we were surprised and extremely upset with the professionals, especially those at the high school who had done such an about-face. It was the height of hypocrisy, this change of mind without even meeting with us, but this was more or less what we had experienced through the many years of John's earlier education. In previous cases, we had gone along with the professionals. We felt that, after all, they should know what was right. This was different. As John's mother, I decided we would not accept a unilateral decision.

Taking time from my work, I locked myself in a private office and prepared to do battle with both the school and the DMR. After several hours of making telephone calls, I finally convinced the DMR that John should be retested. The testing would take place at one of their work sites and would be for five days, not the one day originally allotted for it. We did not feel that John, or any child really, could be evaluated properly on the basis of one day's experience. The DMR also agreed to hold open the sheltered workshop until all the results of John's tests were evaluated. This was much more than I had ever expected to get out of the DMR.

Both of us then sat down with John and tried to get the message across to him that his entire future depended on this evaluation. We were convinced that since he had already held a job or two in the community, he could do it again. We had to ignore the pressure we might be putting on John. This was a rare second chance, and our message to him was, essentially, "Don't blow it, kid."

When the test results were ready, the three of us met with DMR staff and counselors from the school. The evaluation was reviewed, and the DMR counselors were amazed at the complete turnaround in John's performance. Where in the previous testing he had been considered "noncompetitive" in nearly every area, he now tested out "competitive"—i.e., motivated to work and able to stick to a task through its completion—in just about every aspect of the food-services test. The DMR now felt he could and should be considered a candidate for a regular job in the food service area, such as in a restaurant. John was assigned to a pizza restaurant with a job coach to help him adjust. He subsequently was able to graduate from the school. He got an apartment of his own, which he still shares with another young man.

John's job ended when the restaurant went out of business. His father, his vocational coach at the time, was able to find him another job at a diner, and he worked there for several months. It was a only part-time job, at minimum wage and with no benefits, like most of the jobs for young people in John's category.

We then heard of a dishwashing job at an executive cafeteria. This job was at least thirty hours a week, with a starting wage of seven dollars an hour and benefits. It was a great opportunity, and we felt that John had a shot. My husband took John for an interview with the manager, a very pleasant man who, despite little experience working with people with disabilities, was willing to give John a chance. The cafeteria was very busy, and they did not have time or the ability to train or work with someone who could not keep up. John worked for a week on a trial basis and then, with the manager's approval, started full-time.

After John had been on the job about four weeks, however, the manager called us and said that John was having difficulty. He was becoming unstrung emotionally and was not able to keep up with the work load. They apparently served a large number of lunches. The dirty dishes came in fast and furious during the two-hour lunch period and everyone had to keep up the pace or the whole system fell apart. My husband went in and worked with John for several days to see just what was happening. It seemed that there were several things working against John. First of all, the kitchen was extremely hot, dishwashers had to stand in water, and the dishes coming out of the dryer were so hot that your fingers would tingle for days afterward if you handled them without gloves. In addition, other people on the line were not holding up their own ends, and this made the pressure on John even greater.

My husband spoke to the manager about all of this. He asked whether, if we could procure a trained job coach from the local DMR, the manager would be willing to work with John a little longer. The manager was agreeable, so we called the DMR.

We remembered the difficulty we had had with them before, but this time they were delighted to help and gave us a job coach within twenty-four hours. (It turned out that they had been trying to get an "in" at this company to place clients and had not been successful. So they took this as an opportunity to do a little P.R. and get their foot in the door.) The job coach was unable to solve John's problems, however. He did not know John and had never worked in a kitchen before. In any case, he did not know how to deal with John's emotional problems and only, I felt, aggravated the situation. The DMR, of course, had a different point of view. They felt that John was overwhelmed with the job; that he was placed in a job beyond his capabilities; and that he should not have been there to begin with.

Again we had a difference of opinion with the DMR, but this time it worked to our advantage. Because the job market for people in John's category was bad, the DMR felt that John would have a hard time competing and suggested that we apply for disability for him. We had not done this in the past because we always felt that he would be able to support himself. Now we were beginning to have our own doubts. We were approaching the age of retirement and were concerned about how were we going to provide for John if he could not keep a full- or even a part-time job. If he could work at minimum wage for only twelve hours a week, he would never be able to support himself, nor would he ever be eligible for medical or other benefits. So we followed the DMR's recommendation. They wrote the report that got John approved for disability. And because it was made retroactive for the previous year, John immediately received a sizable check.

John has now been receiving disability payments from Social Security and state welfare payments for almost two years. He is also covered by Medicare. We feel that we have provided for his future, and that's all we can do. We still would like John to work out there in a paying job. He needs that for his own morale. He could still handle a job at a supermarket, bagging, or a job at a fast-food restaurant in their food-prep department. But those jobs are either not currently available or very difficult to find, and employers are going to take the applicant with the better qualifications.

For the time being, John volunteers at the home for the aged where he started out seven years ago. He is well liked there. They feel that he is doing an good job, that he gives his all. Once, in the past year, we received a phone call from the DMR saying that John was becoming emotional on the job—teary-eyed—and he couldn't express his feelings enough to say what his problem was or what might be causing his upset. We were able to work out what was bothering him, but the people at the home were very concerned. They like John and want him to continue to be a volunteer, but they don't have the time to deal with his emotions. So we have to keep an eye out so that John can continue to work there.

That's where we stand now. We have felt right from the beginning that John belonged on the outside. We still feel that he does not belong in a sheltered workshop. He is now out in the world with people, helping, smiling, making someone's day, and this is where he belongs—this is something he's capable of doing. He's in the community. He has friends. He entertains and is invited out by many people. Although he still needs counseling, and he still needs support from his family, he handles most of his affairs himself. He's succeeding, and in his own way he's happy.

Sometimes we wonder whether the DMR or we were right. The way things have turned out, maybe we weren't right. We have our doubts. But we know we can only try to do the best we can. We've worked on this together for nearly thirty-four years, and we hope that we'll be around for a while longer to give John the advice and reassurance he still needs.

The lesson we learned as parents was that one should never take "no" for the final answer until all avenues have been explored. Mental health professionals are very busy people, and sometimes rules and procedure and even costs get in the way of their judgment. It takes love and understanding of a young person's problems and desires to know just how far he can go.

And when the chips are down, it takes extreme tenacity. Stick to your guns; it is not impossible to fight city hall. It just means that you have to fight harder for what you believe in. In the end, it is well worth it.

At this time, John is working part-time at a fast-food restaurant. He has adjusted very well to the new job, with the support of a coach. He has expanded his social activities to include going to small dinner parties (he loves to cook), attending some classes offered by the school, and taking part in occasional dance parties. He walks for exercise and recreation and attends some sporting events. He is still involved with many family functions and is still interested in what his former classmates, relatives, and family friends are doing. He uses the telephone like a lifeline to others.

He is happy.

8 • EMOTIONALLY BLOCKED: LARRY PERELLI

born May 8, 1964

Larry Perelli, who came to Ives at age five, died in his sleep in February of his twenty-third year. After many years of what had appeared to be negative achievement and feelings of failure, he had been on the verge of a happier life. He was gaining some control of himself. He was receiving praise at work from his workshop supervisor and at home from his mother and stepfather. For the first time he was feeling some solid success. He had been accepted in a group home and was joyfully preparing to move into comparatively independent living. The autopsy revealed no identifiable cause for his death.

When Larry was four-and-a-half, his pediatricians had referred him to the Yale Child Study Center for diagnosis because of his delay in motor and speech development and his problems in emotional behavior.

Larry's mother, in a series of interviews, displayed perplexity at her son's difficult behavior. She said that he had changed from a well-behaved child to one often out of control. Complicating whatever innate problems Larry had was a chaotic and emotionally charged home life. His infancy and toddlerhood had been rendered confusing, distressing, and probably frightening by the conflict between his divorced parents, and by the strained relationship between his mother and maternal grandmother, with whom Mrs. Perelli and Larry then lived. The evaluations at Yale determined that Larry was an emotionally disturbed boy of basically average intelligence whose cognitive functioning was impaired by his personality disorder. He was extremely anxious and fearful and was beset with preoccupations and confusion of thinking that manifested themselves in odd, idiosyncratic associations to objects, pictures, and phrases. It was not clear whether some degree of inborn predisposition to deviational development had existed in Larry from early on, but it was clear that the adults responsible for him were unable to create a favorable child-rearing environment, and that he had experienced emotional deprivation and trauma in an inconsistent, turbulent environment. Autistic and psychotic features in his behavior made the outlook for the future uncertain.

The autistic component in Larry's personality lay in his "unreachableness," his imperviousness to social contact. He related minimally to people, with no awareness of the impact of his behavior on others. Although he talked incessantly, it was rarely *to* anyone, with little conversational give-and-take. He was a dramatic example of the heterogeneity of autism—a mixture of normality and apparent intelligence, yet totally removed, as if by a wall, from social relationships.

In spite of his disturbances, Larry showed an ability to relate to the psychologist and so was referred to a child psychiatrist for treatment. His mother accepted this referral and seemed eager for the assistance. Larry, at five, began a treatment that continued for three years, with some interruptions because of changes in therapists. (He had three therapists in the three-year period.) At the same time, his doctor at the Yale Child Study Center referred him to the Ives School for his educational needs.

Larry was a puzzling mixture: intelligent and able to relate to people and the environment, he had sudden violent, out-of-control outbursts of screaming, racing around the room destroying everything in his path, grabbing teachers, mouthing or biting shoulders or breasts, repetitive swearing, and running out of the classroom. When these episodes occurred, Larry's teacher would hold him firmly, but gently. Sometimes she might need the help of another teacher for a few minutes to help him calm down. She would take him to the "isolation" room, where she would help him to regain control of himself. There never seemed to be a specific cause for these outbursts.

Because of his behavior, Larry spent his first year at Ives largely apart from other children, in a classroom with one teacher. He joined his class only for snack time, and even this often ended in chaos—spilled juice, much mopping up and negative critical comments from the other children. He would often bolt out of the classroom, and his teacher would have to pursue him and return him to the isolation of his individualized program. It is an indication of his responsiveness that when so removed, he would become frightened and then winningly obedient, saying: "Are you angry with me? Don't be angry with me! I'll be good!"

By his second year at Ives, Larry had developed enough self-confidence and inner control to remain in the classroom with other children. In certain ways he had a quick intelligence, and on his good days he could outperform his classmates. By the end of his second year, he had mastered simple addition and subtraction and could read in a beginning first-grade reader. He initially refused to write, and when he finally attempted to form letters, he reversed many of them. He did very well with puzzles and loved to build with blocks or play with trucks. He also was able to use the outdoor play equipment appropriately.

At Ives (and throughout his life) Larry was, in a way, his own worst enemy. He was a bright little boy, and when he was in good shape he mastered beginning academics—reading, math, and spelling—more easily than others in his class. But he was at the mercy of his uncontrollable emotions and could learn nothing when he was in an uproar.

Larry remained at the Ives preschool for five years, until he was ten, when he went to a residential treatment center. At thirteen, he entered the local special education high school, where he was placed in the communications disorder section. He was soon transferred to the higher-functioning group there.

Larry was tested for that program. The results described him at thirteen-and-a-half as having a mental age of eight years, six months. The psychological summary concluded that in all academic skills he showed an immature and concrete approach, meaning that he was weak in abstract reasoning. He had special difficulty in visual-motor integration; he was weak in sound-symbol integration, and he relied on structure and form to decode words in reading. He was reading on a third-grade, eighth-month level, and his math ability was on a second-grade level.

There were nine children in the higher-functioning group of the program, and Larry's performance was among the highest. Each child sat at a desk somewhat removed from the other eight, creating a feeling of privacy for each child, combined with a warmth of togetherness. There was one main teacher and an aide. The classroom routine was highly structured, yet each child was working on his own program and at his own speed.

When Larry was sixteen, his biological father insisted on seeing him. He had remarried, had two sons close to Larry's age, and was living in the same town. Mrs. Perelli agreed to this and set up a schedule of weekend visits. For the first visit, Larry's father took him out to dinner with his two other sons. Larry, wild with excitement, raced around the restaurant, and the two half-brothers followed his lead. The father managed to quiet Larry down, and afterward Larry began spending whole weekends with his father and stepmother.

By seventeen, Larry had made great progress at school. Academically, he was high-functioning compared to the rest of his group. He used a calculator and read on a third-grade level. But although he had improved a great deal in his ability to control his behavior, he was still unpredictable, and at times he exhibited inappropriate behavior and excessively repetitious conversation. Throughout high school, Larry lived at home. Although things were better there, and his mother was pleased with Larry's teachers and the school, she found keeping Larry at home was still a trial.

At eighteen, Larry was retested by his public school system's psychologist as part of the normal procedure for assessing "special problem" cases. The results confirmed his placement in the communication disorders program. At that time, Larry's teacher had detected that his eyesight was terrible and recommended that he see an ophthalmologist and obtain better glasses. At this same time, Larry's mother had given birth to another child, and the plans to see an ophthalmologist were scrapped in the face of Larry's bad reaction to the new baby. The arrival of the baby apparently had made him even more susceptible to losing control, and his mother felt that neither she nor the ophthalmologist could have managed him successfully during an eye exam.

On the advice of Larry's teachers, he might have returned to a residential treatment center, but he remained in the communication disorders program after the Planning and Placement Team advised that he stay in one consistent, low-key program. Thinking of the future, his teachers felt that because Larry was high-functioning, he would eventually do well in a structured group home.

In his high school vocational class, Larry was unable to concentrate on the job. He talked erratically and nonstop and often seemed to be totally absorbed in his own world. His eyes—he was slightly cockeyed—were always moving, yet he never looked at anyone directly. His hands were never still, and he stopped work every few minutes to change the radio station. The vocational teacher could not let Larry work independently and checked on him every few moments. Larry's tension and hyperexcitement often seemed on the border of becoming un-controllable, yet he responded to correction and would calm down if a teacher told him to.

During his last year in high school, Larry was in group therapy at school. He also began therapy with an out-of-town psychiatrist whom he liked. As a result, he improved in the consistency and control of his behavior. That summer he worked as an aide at a special education camp and got good reports from his supervisor.

Larry graduated from his special education high school at twenty-two, and after an evaluation at the local rehabilitation center, he was placed in its workshop. At first, erratic and constantly asking questions or screaming, Larry was often impossible to control. He once disappeared from the workroom and was discovered by his frantic supervisor lying in the street, head on the curb, long legs out in the street, inviting destruction by the next car.

Larry's caseworkers set up a highly structured program for him, consisting of behavioral contracts that established limits, rewards, and daily objectives. Through these contracts, Larry's obnoxious and erratic behavior lessened. His improvement was such that he was accepted in a group home, much to the pride and delight of him and his family. Then, for no apparent reason, he died one night, quietly, in his sleep.

The tragedy of Larry lies not only in his early death but also in his day-to-day struggle to control himself and permit his intelligent functioning to show. Yet, despite his difficulties with emotional upheaval, he *did* improve, and it is sad that death came to rob him of the fruition of his desire just as it seemed attainable: semi-independence, living in a group home, working in his sheltered workshop.

9 • MUTE AND ANGRY: ERIC THOMAS
born May 23, 1965

Eric came to the Ives School in the late spring, when he was four years old. He was referred to Ives by the Yale Child Study Center, to which he had been sent by the Yale-New Haven Hospital Pediatric Outpatient Clinic because of his lack of speech. Aside from speech, his development was considered normal. He sat at six months, and stood and walked at twelve months. He had made baby sounds at one year, but only between the ages of three and four had he begun to say a few words: "mama," "eat," "baby," "tata," and "no." Otherwise he made little effort to communicate either with or without words.

Eric tended to play alone and be in his own world a great deal of the time. Although he loved music and tried to dance to television at home, when children his own age came to play, he shut himself in his room and rocked on his bed. He was able to play normally with trucks but just looked at most other toys. He was fascinated by noises, particularly of cars starting.

Eric appeared jealous of his siblings and had severe tantrums. His mother had a history of mental illness, for which she had been hospitalized several times. Eric's brothers and sisters helped to take care of him five days a week, yet undoubtedly Mrs. Thomas's uncertain mental health had made adjustment harder for him.

The physician at the Yale Child Study Center described

Eric as a well-developed, handsome boy whom she found very difficult to test. He clung to the materials he liked and wailed when they were taken away. Although he vocalized in an expressive, animated jargon in which some sounds could be distinguished—"whee," "tata," and "there it is"—he totally ignored questions and commands. His self-absorption and detachment from the environment made him almost impossible to reach. The frequent changes in his behavior without any obvious outside reason, as if he were responding to an inner stimulus, made him even more of a challenge.

Through the testing, Eric was found to have well-developed fine-motor skills. He liked and clung to pegs, blocks, and crayons. He could build a tower of five blocks and find a hidden toy. He also scribbled.

Eric's test results were affected by his imperviousness. He was successful at a twenty-one-month to twenty-four-month level on some test items, and this seemed to indicate that he possessed at least a minimum of ability. The physician who tested Eric summarized her assessment by stating that Eric had an abnormality of personality development, probably inborn, known (at that time) as congenital autism.

When Eric came to the Ives School, he was a little boy with a snub nose and a cherubically round face. He had coffee-colored skin and a beguiling smile, which, however, was not aimed at anybody or anything. He was endearing, but for the most part he represented a defeat for the teachers at Ives. His smile and unfocused affability were at first mistaken for responsiveness to others, but he was soon found to be surrounded emotionally by an "invisible wall" that made communication difficult. He shared this personality trait of "imperviousness" with several other children at Ives. Eric's characteristic behavior was to walk, compulsively yet apparently aimlessly, around the play yard, with his head cocked to one side, smiling.

He never played with any of the other children or with outdoor equipment unless supervised and, usually, assisted by a teacher.

Midway through his second year, Eric began to show marked regression. He had spells of trancelike abstraction alternated with hyperactive aggression and fits of temper. He became aggressive toward his classmates and started having tantrums. Twice he ran unnoticed out of the classroom. He was found by a frightened teacher each time, wandering around the building. When Eric was put on medication to treat this behavior, he became less aggressive and less prone to tantrums. He was still unmanageable at home, however, and ran away several times. Once he was found by the railroad tracks and another time down by the harbor. Because his behavior began to exceed that which Ives was capable of handling, he was referred to the autistic unit of a state hospital in a neighboring town. There were no openings at the state hospital, however, so, pending more appropriate placement, Eric remained at Ives.

By this time, Eric could sort by color, shape, and size. He could string beads, place pegs in a pegboard, and color, left-handed, in scribbles. His school reports nevertheless still described him as out of touch with reality.

When Eric was six, he transferred from Ives to the communication disorders section of the public school special education program. He remained in that program until he graduated at twenty-one.

Eric was tested several times over the course of his schooling. One test described him as a healthy and cute twelve-year-old boy who was functioning far below age level in all respects. He was described as inattentive, impulsive, hyperactive, and very unsure of his perceptions of the environment. He required support and encouragement in order to respond to the test questions and was so confused that when he did respond, he often gave several responses to each one.

The examiner concluded that he was functionally retarded

in all areas measured by the test. He had a maturational age of three years, six months, with an IQ of 36. The tests also found that he was particularly impaired in auditory sequencing, meaning that other people's speech came to him as a jumbled series of noises from which he could not extract meaning. This neurological impairment affected his thought processes and emotional control and perhaps made his rages, inability to adjust to change, and frustration understandable.

His greatest strength lay in his ability to follow visual cues, which helped him make sense of his environment. But the inability to understand speech or to express himself even minimally caused great frustration for Eric and exaggerated his high anxiety level. He needed supervision and remedial help, needs being addressed by his special education program.

Eric continued to have problems as an adolescent. By fifteen, he had a history of violence against women and had beaten up several teachers, including his own teacher, a woman. He had to be watched carefully by the staff, and a male teacher's aide accompanied him at all times and stood behind his desk in class.

Eric still frequently exploded into wild tantrums, and when he did, he had to be removed to a small, padded isolation room, where he was locked in until his violent anger subsided. During these spells, he kicked and hammered the door and occasionally loosened the padlock. He brought his rage under control only after being told repeatedly that he would not be let back into his classroom until he calmed down.

According to his school file, Eric was working on basic tools of learning. He had mastered some sign language and could understand simple oral directions and questions if they were given with gestures from the teacher. He could sign the action words "walk," "stand," "swim," "hop," "eat," "drink," "blow," "break," and "pull," but he did none of this spontaneously. He responded to "open," "close," "pick up," "turn off," "turn on," "color," "draw" (a circle but not a triangle or square), "fold," "pour," "sand," "sweep," and "mop." He could use a pencil, sponge, scissors, and crayons correctly. He could color and print with teacher participation. In gross-motor training, he could roll, crawl, hop, and skip, and with help, he did exercises in imitating physical postures (i.e., copying the teacher's gestures or movements). His social skills were minimal. On a good day, he could be part of a group and listen and obey with teacher supervision. His visual-motor skills consisted of the ability, again with prompting, to match pictures, reproduce a pegboard pattern, string beads according to a pattern, put two halves together, and trace. In early pre-vocational classes, he had learned to water houseplants.

Later, Eric entered vocational classes structured for the lowest functioning group, with two teachers and eight students. The classes began each day with one of the teachers saying and signing "Hello." Eric could sometimes repeat this in a hoarse voice, but primarily he signed. All eight young adults were asked to follow the basic directions: "wash hands," "dry hair," "brush teeth," and "wait." After each of the eight students performed one of these actions, the teacher rewarded him by saying: "You earned a raisin for good waiting" or for "brushing your teeth." Later in the day, the students performed manual tasks, such as painting blocks of wood. Eric was consistently able to stick to his job and do it well.

The director of Eric's vocational program said that Eric had definite skill in carpentry and woodworking. This seemed to bear out his early evaluation of good coordination in fine-motor skills. The possibility that Eric might be able to pursue a vocation, however, was limited by his history of emotional instability and violent behavior, which, even though it had improved, made normal placement in a sheltered workshop very doubtful.

During these years, Eric's family was very supportive.

Eric's mother was serious and concerned. She kept all of Eric's medical appointments for shots, checkups, and dental work, and she spent her Aid to Dependent Children allotment on sensible food for a well-balanced diet for all of her family. Her niece-in-law, girlfriend, and brother-in-law helped with Eric, but stopped as he grew older and more aggressive. Mrs. Thomas's father, sister, son, and grandson took turns giving her a few hours or a weekend off from caring for Eric. There were times when Eric's bouts of violence and running away drove her to think about putting him in an institution, but neither she nor the family ever contemplated this seriously.

After graduation from his special education high school, Eric was placed in a sheltered workshop program, where he continued to receive job training and to try to improve social and verbal communication and control of his behavior. Although Eric often complied with instructions quietly and willingly, at the same time he communicated a sense of tautly controlled violence that might erupt at any moment. He would stand and raise his arms, gesturing with his hands, up and down, simultaneously looking at the sky and seeming to address an unseen presence with incomprehensible gibberish. He would frequently try to parrot the last word or phrase of other people's sentences. His enunciation was slurred and indecipherable.

At the workshop, Eric's control of his violent behavior continued to improve. He saw a psychiatrist at a state mental health clinic and was on medication, which was monitored at the workshop. When he was in control of himself, he did well in jobs which involved fine-motor skills, but the instability of his behavior interfered with his productivity. Close supervision was required to keep him on task. He became confused and disoriented easily. He had one particular chair in one special place at his workbench. If this familiar routine was changed, he had a temper tantrum. Usually in the first hour after his arrival, he was visibly upset, sullen, perspiring, and in a physiological state that his supervisor felt was due to a general frustration. The first hour at work he was often allowed to sit quietly listening to the radio. After this, he was able to settle down to his job.

Eric's future is uncertain. To send him to an institution (as had been expected when he was in high school) would be disastrous for him and an admission of defeat for his family and all who were involved with him. His family has been concerned about his aggression and would like to see him in a group home, and they feel encouraged that this might be possible. His name is high on the list for a group home where he could be managed and contained appropriately. Certainly this is solid progress and success compared to institutionalization, which had seemed inevitable at a younger age.

In October 1987, at twenty-two, Eric was tested at the Yale Child Study Center. His mother could not attend, so the Vineland was omitted, and he was only tested on the WAIS-R and ABC.

WAIS-R
Verbal IQ: 51   Performance IQ: 51   Full Scale IQ: 46

VINELAND
(Mrs. Thomas was unavailable to answer the questions for this test.)

ABC
101: Probably autistic

The psychologist observed:

> During the administration of the Wechsler Adult Intelligence Scale-Revised, Eric asked for water several times, drank it and made a squealing sound. He evidenced repeti-

tive and stereotypic behaviors, lip-smacking and raising his arms when he was excited. He repeated the last words in an echolalic fashion, and, in doing motor tasks, his coordination seemed quite awkward. His full scale IQ was 46, classified as in the severe deficit range of mental retardation with no difference in verbal and performance. Eric . . . showed relative strength in placing a series of pictures in logical sequence, which shows ability to comprehend a situation using nonverbal reasoning in which anticipation, visual organization, and temporal sequencing are involved.

Dr. Volkmar said of Eric's results: "Eric, with an IQ of 46, is the most typically autistic [of the children in this book]."

IV • WHERE DOES THIS LEAVE US? PARENTS, TEACHERS, AND CHILDREN

The original purpose of this book was to present case studies of children with varying autistic behaviors whom the author taught and followed to adulthood. One, Larry, died in his sleep at twenty-three, but the eight others vary in age at the time of this writing from thirty to thirty-six. These nine stories and the accounts of six of the parents would lead the reader to some bittersweet conclusions. The nine children are fairly representative of the general population of autistics—neither as severely impaired as the most disabled nor as brilliant in astonishing ways as some autistic *savants*. If this book and the stories in it presented the status quo, then the inference to be drawn about the future of autistic adults would be at once encouraging—intensive education and one-on-one care of the autistic child through to adulthood does ameliorate and adjust autistic behaviors—and equally discouraging, for no matter what the improvement, the young autistic adult remains basically the same, handicapped by problems in relating to the world.

But this book, fortunately, does not present the status quo. There are continuing advances in medical research and various new methods of treatment for autistics, and although there is no cure, the outlook now is brighter than it ever has been. In fact, there are so many promising new treatments available that some experts suggest families explore any new therapy they think might have an effect. Ruth Sullivan, director of the Autism Services Center in Huntington, West Virginia, mother of Joseph Sullivan, one of the models for the character of Raymond in the movie *Rain Man*, feels encouraged. She has said, "Some very exciting things have been happening—we've never seen progress to this extent."[1] So, where do we stand now? In what way is the current situation better for teachers, for parents, and for autistic children now grown to adulthood?

Teachers

A great deal has been learned about autism and childhood developmental disorders since the 1960s. No longer is the teaching of developmentally disabled children nebulous or a matter of guesswork. The special education field has become better delineated, and its goals have been clarified. Teaching materials and techniques are constantly improving and expanding. Years of clinical and teaching experience and numerous longitudinal studies of autistic children have led to the acceptance of the concept of an underlying organic, though still enigmatic, etiology of autism.[2] In contrast to the controversy of the early 1960s, the most widely acknowledged opinion now is that the origin of autism is not largely psychogenic, but that autism has neurochemical and other organic causes and, in some instances, genetic origins that express themselves in psychological dysfunction.

The variety and degree of the abnormalities of behavior and impairments of function found in autistic children are considerable. For instance, CAT scans at Yale found left-hemisphere deficiencies in the brains of some autistic children.

About Kim, another model for Raymond in *Rain Man*, Daniel Christensen, medical director of the Western Institute of Neuropsychiatry at the University of Utah, said: "[Kim] has a photographic memory, but no way to minimize stimuli. Brain scans show an absence of the bundle of nerve fibers that connect the two halves of the brain."[3] The great variation in the syndromes of autism and atypical development underscore the importance of precision in diagnosis. Progress in the diagnosis and definition of autism and its related syndromes has been an important factor in the growth and implementation of theories on teaching autistic children. The specificity of diagnosis directly affects the choice of teaching techniques and materials available to the present-day teacher.

In the 1960s, teachers, however well educated, had to teach autistic children with intuition, and often with handmade materials. As described earlier, the teachers at Ives used innovative paper cutouts of red, blue, green, and yellow squares, triangles, and circles, block pattern designs, etc. None had used such materials before and all had to learn, from scratch, how, when, and why to use them and other novel techniques. Teachers now have textbooks and workbooks especially geared for the developmentally disabled, as well as other teaching aids such as computers, cassettes, television, video-cassette recorders, and copying machines. A generation of teachers has developed and refined teaching approaches such as behavior modification, signing, mainstreaming, pre-vocational and vocational training, special physical education, music, art, and recreation. Special educators have been joined by occupational therapists, physical therapists, speech and language specialists, music and dance therapists, and specialists in other disciplines in addressing the difficult tasks of communicating with and enhancing the general learning potential and otherwise solving or alleviating developmental problems of autistic children. Even with transdisciplinary, multiple, coordinated teaching methods and improved teaching materials and strategies, there remains a constant need for teachers and their colleagues to be able to individualize their materials and approaches to a particular child. Resourcefulness, flexibility, knowing a child well, and having the courage to modify and question existing methods remain crucial for the most effective education and therapy.

Teachers now have some idea of what to expect when dealing with the developmentally handicapped. Since the passage of the Education of the Handicapped Act in 1970, the courses in child development given at teachers' colleges have paid progressively more attention to the educational problems of the handicapped. There is also now an educated stratum of sophisticated and well-trained professionals employed in or serving the programs available to the developmentally handicapped, from the directors of these programs, who are often themselves specialists, to social workers who back up the teachers through liaison with parents, and psychologists who perform and score developmental testing. In addition, the physicians at child development and mental health clinics and in private practice are now able to identify specific developmental problems that were poorly understood a generation ago.

Many teachers today also have the advantage of a state-regulated, federally funded plan, developed in the 1980s, to educate educationally handicapped children as well as older preschool and school-age children in "Birth to Three" programs. The thrust of this program is early intervention, and its intention is to give everyone—child, teacher, and parents—a head start. The earlier the intervention, the better the chance for improving the autistic child's modification of his or her disabilities, for effective teaching, and for parents' informed coping with autistic behaviors.

The student who today contemplates teaching autistic children has a good chance of making a realistic decision. She or he has the opportunity to observe a variety of classes and programs for the developmentally handicapped: private schools (nursery school to high school), public school special education programs, state-sponsored service centers, and early intervention programs. From these, the student can assess whether she or he has the capabilities and personality traits needed to be a successful teacher of the autistic.

But all the progress made in the last twenty-five years still has not made it an easy job. Anyone starting off on a career of teaching autistic or other developmentally handicapped children often feels lost, not knowing which way to turn, where to go, or what to do. Physical endurance, emotional stability, flexibility, ability and willingness to improvise, and a respect for the value of one's own intuition, are all needed to work with developmental disabilities. This kind of teaching is not everyone's cup of tea.

Two examples of rather promising methods of treatment for autism that have developed recently are *facilitated communication* and *auditory training*. Facilitated communication was first developed by an Australian, Rosemary Crossley, and her colleagues at the Dignity Through Education and Language Communication Centre in Melbourne. Brought to this country by Douglas Biklen, a professor at Syracuse University,[4] it involves using a *common communicator* (a small electronic typing device with a dot-matrix tape output) on which the autistic person types answers to questions asked by a *facilitator*. Facilitators work with each autistic person on a one-to-one basis and "facilitate" by lightly supporting the autistic person's typing hand (or, in some cases, placing a hand gently on his or her shoulder or back), while he or she types the answers. The treatment itself involves a series of questions and other strategies carefully developed and outlined, and seems to offer hope to some of the most severely speech-impaired autistics. There is still controversy over facilitated communication, however, as the possibility of excessive manipulation by the facilitator can put positive results in doubt.

Auditory training, developed by Dr. Guy Berard in France, opens up another avenue of treatment. This approach focuses on the fact that many autistics have hyperacute hearing, which leads to faulty auditory processing of sounds and makes even simple sounds, such as a speaking voice, unbearable. The technique uses audiograms and electronic sound filters to help identify and modulate, sometimes even remedy, hearing hyper-sensitivity.[5]

There is continuing interest and research in the neuro-chemistry of the brain in autistic individuals, and the literature abounds with new and updated studies. Strategies currently used in neurobiological research on psychiatric disorders can be grouped into four types: (a) studies of neurotransmitters and related enzymes; (b) measurement of neurotransmitter reception; (c) neuroendocrine studies; and (d) brain-imaging studies.[6] The most extensively studied neurotransmitters hy-pothesized to be involved in childhood neuropsychiatric disor-ders are serotonin, dopamine, and norepinephrine. Emphasis has been placed on these three neurotransmitters because of their role in predicting behavioral phenomena. Measurements of their metabolites in cerebrospinal fluid, blood, and urine have been extensively assayed. Neuroendocrine and enzyme studies are also the focus of attention in autism and other neuropsychiatric disorders of childhood. Brain-imaging stud-ies—e.g., computerized axial tomography (CAT scans), mag-netic resonance imaging (MRI), and positron emission tomogra-phy (PET)—are being extensively employed to examine neuroanatomical structure.

As these methods of study and treatment become refined, they will have an impact on teachers and teaching methods. Even now, they are raising questions and beginning to cause change. The basic necessary approach to teaching, however, has not changed: Each child's strengths must be analyzed and used.

The Parents

The central purpose of this book has been to show a group of autistic children and the problems faced by their families. The parents—after years of enduring bitter struggle, minor hopes, major disappointments, and some victories and of dealing with pressures that can lead to quarrels, disagreement, resentment, and sometimes divorce—are facing a comparatively improved situation, but only comparatively. These families long ago accepted the fact of their daughters' and sons' multiple impairments. But in their hearts, they hoped for a release from the imprisoning burden of their children's disabilities. Now in their early to mid-thirties, the young people themselves are for the most part only marginally independent, and all but Bill continue to rely on their parents and families in ways that unimpaired people do not.

Although none of the families had the good fortune to be supported by a coordinated-treatment approach over the period of many years when it was needed, their stories show that they, sometimes blindly and by luck, developed out of necessity a way of coping with an autistic child and all the attendant crises. Indecision and ignorance increased their agony. Essentially these families illustrate—effectively in some instances, less so in others—the practical day-to-day progress and setbacks experienced in learning to cope with an autistic child.

The parents' stories illustrate their common problems, the limited answers, and the qualified future possibilities for all of their children. Each of the families—wife, husband, and the other, "normal" children—experienced the pain, embarrassment, and hopelessness of having an autistic child in the family. The following concerns emerge in all of the accounts:

- The shock of realizing that an infant or toddler is different from other babies.

- The search for diagnosis and the realization that there is no treatment other than education and, in some cases, medication, and that there is no cure.

- The search for guidance on management of the child's behavior once the diagnosis is given.

- The necessity of locating a school appropriate for the child's needs.

- The day-to-day stress of living with puzzling, difficult, and often violent behavior.

- The social isolation caused by lack of understanding of a handicapped child. There is inability and unwillingness to entertain at home, either because of family feelings or because the handicapped child cannot tolerate strangers. Siblings are unable to invite friends home.

- The certainty that the mother is trapped. As Karen's mother said, "The buck stops here."

- The need for competent babysitters: Once found, they must be trained to care for a developmentally disabled, perplexing child.

- How to manage vacation time, even a long weekend. One family (not in this group of nine) is taking their first vacation in twenty-two years, because their twenty-two-year-old autistic son is now in a group home.

- Constant pressure to guard the interests of the child. Bureaucratic red tape must be honored in order to get financing, proper educational placement, and such necessities as medical insurance. It is necessary to read the fine print of all relevant state and federal requirements. As the child gets older, the rapidly changing field of pre-vocational and vocational training must be mastered.

- How to finance the staggering cost of clinics, doctors, therapists, medicine, and home care.

- The need for counseling for all the family, including siblings.

- Living arrangements for the over-twenty-one, developmentally disabled adult. The choice is between group homes and more independent situations, or keeping the young adult at home.

- Social life of the child. How does one handle the isolation of the child who usually cannot play with his neighborhood peers, and who when older is left out of normal teenage social activities?

- What to do with a sexually maturing disabled adult?

- The ever-present worry about how to make sure that the semi-independent autistic adult is cared for appropriately after the parents can no longer do so. Guardianship? Stand-by guardianship? Proper estate planning and wills? What is the answer?

The dilemma of acceptance is acute. Most developmentally disabled children are deceptively normal in appearance and often handsome as infants and toddlers, as were all nine children in this group. The superficial normality can hinder parents' acceptance of their child as he or she truly is, and affect their ability to handle pragmatic day-to-day living with autism or autistic behavior.

Everyone with a developmentally disabled child feels bitterness, disbelief, and bewilderment at first. The disabilities often are contradictory, with the autistic component being the most difficult to understand. It is normal to feel lost and not to know where to turn for a solution. Parents experience love mixed with hate, anger, black despair, and rebellion that they should be saddled with such a hopeless problem. And there is guilt: guilt over their feelings that they might be responsible for the child's condition; guilt over the common conscious wish that the problem, or the child, would disappear or die.

Acceptance of the child and his or her handicap, no matter how agonizing, slow, and partial at first, sets a parent free to act as a fighter and advocate for the child. Sometimes parents realize that they have a need for the developmentally disabled child/adult to remain just as he or she is: The parent would miss the child should he or she suddenly be "better" or "get cured." In a bittersweet way, such parents love the child as he is. Siblings of autistics often say that having an autistic brother or sister has added a special quality to their lives—an experience that they would not do without. Interestingly, some of these "normal" siblings choose to go into the helping professions.

The Children Grown Up

The stories contained in this book demonstrate that autistic persons can accommodate their behavior sufficiently so that many of them can become comparatively self-sufficient adults. Bill Kolinski is completely independent. All autistic and other developmentally handicapped people have talents and abilities that, when encouraged, can help them grow from emotionally distant young children to adults who work in workshops or jobs in the community. As is apparent from the stories in this book, autistic adults can fill a variety of jobs: They work as janitors and clerks (collating and filing), do simple assembly work, and work in fast-food or other restaurants as dishwashers (Tom) and simple cooks. Polly has a responsible job in the kitchen of a fast-food restaurant. Bill is assistant chef at a restaurant at Disney World. They can be aides in nursing homes, as John is, or gardeners in landscaping services, or baggers in grocery stores. Others work in more complicated jobs. Temple Grandin is one of the best-known examples.

Author of many articles, such as "Needs of High-Functioning Teenagers and Adults with Autism (Tips From a Recovered Autistic)" and author of the book *Emergence: Labeled Autistic*, she is now an assistant professor of animal science at Colorado State University.[7] One young male autistic adult who graduated *cum laude* from an Ivy League college is now a computer programmer.

It is a measure of victory over their disability that many autistics can earn salaries, work with normal coworkers, live away from home in groups, and have some social life in the community.

But although there has been improvement in services and a growing emphasis on helping autistic people live and work with normal peers, the ideal is not always the reality. Each of the young adults in this book has had serious difficulties along the way, even when the appropriate services were in place. Jimmy was excluded from his bus for unacceptable behavior (masturbation) and had to go by special car for four-hour stints at his workshop, instead of the usual eight; his mother had nowhere else to turn for help. In 1992, however, this changed. Jimmy is now back in his eight-hour program and on the bus. John came close to failing his tests in fast-food services and being dropped by the Department of Vocational Rehabilitation. Thanks to his mother's fighting an entire government bureaucracy for him, he was given a second chance. And so on.

Even with the best services that can be offered generally, society must still deal with these people as individuals. Some manage well enough that they do not appear markedly different from others in their age group, even when some problems of social functioning and intimacy remain. Nevertheless, after all their schooling, autistic adults often read and do math on only a second- to fourth-grade level. And each one who can verbalize his feelings is conscious of being different, somehow not "normal." John once said that he hated his explosions, losing his control, and wondered why it happened to him. Polly describes herself matter-of-factly as mentally retarded, but she cries about it, and cries when her retarded friends cry. Karen denies feeling different from other people, yet her actions betray her awareness otherwise. Her constant reassurances, repeated echolalically to herself when visiting the author, that she "was not going home now," revealed her joy at being in a new environment.

None of the handicaps of the people in this book will go away. Jimmy will probably never talk, and will have to express himself through sign language and confused attempts at words. He also needs much help controlling his sexual drives. Eric hears sounds mostly as meaningless. Bill is working successfully at Disney World. But he will never be rid of his subtle anxiety centering around personal relationships, and his mother recounts that he was placed as an assistant rather than head chef because he can't handle the pressure. John is puzzled by his outbursts of crying, his tantrums, his intense anxiety in dealing with people. Although working as an aide at a nursing home, he is threatened with losing this volunteer job because of his emotional outbursts. Tom is inarticulate and shy and suffers from an inability to contact or cope with people. Although he works with normal people in a restaurant, he must still be watched over by them.

Each of these people has a high anxiety level that may come partially from their perceptual disabilities, which distort their picture of the environment and interfere with their ability to organize and understand their experiences. Karen's lack of depth perception and visual-motor control showed up in her clumsy attempts to use a push-button telephone. She got the wrong number twice before successfully calling her mother. David must be walked step by step from his bus to the community house and back. He is being trained to find his way and take note of landmarks between the bus stop and his job until he proves that he can do it by himself. At the moment, however,

David is now working in a discount store, where he is supervised by a job coach, and his father still drives him to work.

The hardest thing for these autistic adults to manage is *not* their lack of ability to be with or to talk with other people but the fact that they can only do it in a detached manner. Many often genuinely cannot use speech for communicative purposes. One authority suggests that "autistic children do not fail to represent word meaning in memory"; that is, they know that the letters "d", "o", and "g" mean the same thing as a picture of a dog, but they "fail to use that meaning in the normal way in retrieval or organizational tasks."[8] Most of them find it impossible to understand the feelings of the people around them, so that they often say or do things that are inappropriate. This can cause bewilderment, and sometimes amusement or fear in other people, and sometimes leads to rejection. Like a pebble thrown into the water, creating ever-widening circles, the behavior of autistic people increases their oddness and isolation, and perhaps their loneliness as well.

This book is a plea for understanding of autism. We have white canes, seeing-eye dogs, and Braille for the blind; we have adjusted jobs so that the blind may work out in the community. The deaf have sign language, special captions in sign language on television programs, enhanced-hearing telephones, and hearing aids. They too find jobs that have been adjusted to their handicap. Most of the general, "normal" public are handicapped by their lack of ability to deal with their ignorance about the condition of autism and autistic or autistic-like thinking and conversation. Isn't it time we made a determined effort to educate the public about autistic people so that they are not ruled out of jobs because they "won't fit"? So that we can better understand their thought processes and establish better communication, no longer condemning them to treatment as "odd," even sometimes as "crazy"? Instead, we can welcome the strength of this hitherto unused human potential to our world.

The fact that autistic and atypical disorders comprise a heterogeneous group rather than define a unitary disease makes generalizations about autistics difficult, even hazardous. Their behavior as young children, especially the problems in establishing relationships and social communication, and the problems of anxiety and cognitive confusion, have justified the terms "autism" or "autistic syndrome" in providing a terminological distinction between them and other developmental disabilities and neuropsychiatric disorders. Variations in the severity of the symptoms have been documented repeatedly, as has the variation in findings that accompany the major syndrome: deafness, inborn errors of metabolism, blindness, identifiable brain damage, sensory processing problems, perceptual handicaps, Fragile X syndrome, and many others. Only continued efforts to understand and clarify, through basic and clinical research, are likely to yield information that defines clearly the underlying, and probably multiple, causes of this spectrum of disorders.

Meanwhile, those who live and work with children like the adults represented here may find some comfort in the knowledge that appropriate services, rendered early and sustained over many years, can make a difference in the lives of autistic children and their parents.

NOTES

1. Emily Laber, "Symptoms, Treatments for Autism," *New Haven Advocate*, Jan. 20, 1992.
2. F. R. Volkmar, "Social Development," in D. J. Cohen and A. M. Donnellan, eds., *Handbook of Autism and Pervasive Developmental Disorders* (New York: John Wiley & Sons, 1987), hereinafter cited as Cohen and Donnellan, 41–60.
3. Associated Press, "Real Rain Man Thrives with Film," *New Haven (Conn.) Register*, Feb. 19, 1989, A2.

4. D. Biklen, "Communication Unbound: Autism and Praxis," *Harvard Educational Review* 60(3) (August 1990): 291–314.
5. B. Rimland, "Editor's Notebook: Sound Sensitivity in Autism," *Autism Research Review International* 4(4): 3.
6. G. Anderson and Y. Hoshino, "Neurochemical Studies of Autism," Cohen & Donnellan, 166–91.
7. T. Grandin and M. Scariano, *Emergence: Labelled Autistic* (Novato, Calif.: Arena Press, 1986); T. Grandin, *Needs of High Functioning Teenagers and Adults with Autism (Tips from a Recovered Autistic)* (Dept. of Animal Sciences, Colorado State University, Fort Collins, Col.) 805, 2–3.
8. R. Paul, "Communication," in Cohen & Donnellan, 66.

Appendix A
GROWING IN
AND OUT OF
AN AUTISTIC MIND
by Bill Kolinski

I'd never heard, or at least understood, the word "autistic" until I saw the film *Rain Man*. And though I never remember believing or acting the way Dustin Hoffman did in his award-winning role of Raymond, I have studied the subject some, and come to an understanding of why—in my early childhood—I would have to a lesser degree been labeled as autistic.

Since most kindergarten children are handicapped with language barriers, I thought you might like to know how I have battled my way out of autism to write stories and poetry, earn my bachelor's degree in journalism, and become successful out in the working and social world by claiming my faith.

As far as I can remember back clearly, I did live pretty much in my own idiosyncratic fantasy world. And as goes along with the definition of an autistic child, I remember not communicating much in the way of talking or facial expression.

It was in kindergarten where I remember first being blatantly eccentric and rejecting almost everything they were trying to teach me about dealing with the real world—including playing with my classmates. I prided myself on being independent-minded and using reverse- psychology tactics on my teacher and others, except for my parents. Basically I had no desire or motivation to deal with or adjust to most people and the world around me. I feared the unknown and as a result, change. Not caring what anyone thought of me, I had decided I would be happier making my own rules in the safe bubble of the dream world I had created (or which possessed me), and I wasn't going to let anyone come inside or threaten it.

Once the school nurse told my parents I might be deaf because I didn't raise my hand when I heard the high pitch of her tuning fork during a hearing test. (I heard it very clearly.) I remember thinking it was fun to ignore and fool people like her. I constantly played mind games when people tried to reach me. Sometimes it felt like I was watching life around me on a large TV screen, and I wasn't a part of it.

I was very good at analyzing and understanding people's behavior, including my own. But perhaps due to my excessive shyness and sensitivity, I was afraid of being hurt or rejected by my peers, so I felt like I didn't need any friends. I lacked the will to be accepted or to fight my way out of my trapped mind. So I turned almost fully to a nonreacting, nonjudgmental, intellectual/soulful friend which would please me uncondi-tionally—music.

No one introduced me to any instruments or encouraged me to learn to play, so I've never found my full potential of any talent in music. But I could sit for hours on end listening to and memorizing almost every type of music I heard, down to the finite details of instrumentals and structure of hundreds of songs and classical symphonies. I connected spiritually with music, but I didn't tell anyone.

I had already decided life in general was not as romantic as the stories and visions I interpreted from the music in my out-of-control imagination, so I began allowing my mind to blend the visions with reality to make existence more interest-ing—like many of the early Romantic European poets probably did. I suppose many people who smoke dope or take LSD to alter their senses try to capture the vivid surrealistic sensations with which I perceived the world in my self-absorbed fantasies. I knew what was going on around me and what people expected of me, but since I was unable to grasp the purpose of growing up from one stage to another, I chose not to snap out of my dream world.

I've read that typical autistic children aren't able to really fantasize because of their limited comprehension. And although I remember having a short attention span because I felt hyperactive, and would tune out reality because I didn't find concentrating on my responsibilities important or interesting, when I tuned out I daydreamed about things and ideas, including words. If something like music, passages from books, or places fascinated me, I had a photographic memory.

One of my poet/rock singer idols—the late Jim Morrison—said of his own eccentric behavior, "Let's just say I was testing the bounds of reality. I was curious to see what would happen." That's how I felt.

Sometimes my fantasies would control my mind to the point of on-the-edge irrational fear. One morning I imagined that I would sink into the floor if I got out of bed, and it took me about an hour to muster up the courage to slowly step on it. When I had vivid dreams of someone—a teacher at Ives once—I literally expected them to remember being in the same dream, and was stunned when they told me this is impossible. It was also at this time that I developed a great interest in art—especially drawing.

It was at Ives where they popped my fantasy bubble and forced me to become aware, even self-conscious, of my unpleasant eccentric behavior. All the bottled-up energy due to my withdrawal I would channel out by acting crazy—often deliberately—to get the kind of attention I sought. My cousin, who had just come from Poland, also stabilized me. I taught her to speak English, and she steered me into acting more like a normal American kid.

I did struggle with learning school work, mostly because I couldn't get myself to concentrate. But one of the most important things I learned in the Ives program was to appreciate the purpose for being in school and growing through the various levels of life.

After Ives and through much of public school, I would still occasionally get a kick out of making a fool of myself to get laughs from peers—good or bad. My self-consciousness began to almost possess my mind and emotions like the early fantasies had, and severe shyness resulted. It became what I refer to as "emotional warfare" in high school, where I became crazy about girls and began to stutter. I wanted to make love to every girl in school but couldn't get myself to say hi to them.

In the tenth grade I saw a psychiatrist for my stuttering, and though I loved talking to him, he couldn't give me any advice I didn't already know. It was up to me to conquer my fears of failure (the cause of my stuttering), break through, and go for the gusto. How to exactly go about that, I hadn't yet gotten control of.

This coincided with me beginning to worship my older brother Steve, who to me at the time seemed larger than life—like Jack Kennedy or a movie star. He did just about anything he set his mind to. What many, as myself, only dreamed, he went out and lived fully and with great style. Steve had a daring and charisma about him which made him a center for others, and I wanted to be that ideal center more than anything. I decided to fight and break through self-doubt and shyness and become as much like my brother as I had in me. Socially and academically I didn't get that far. But I dressed more stylishly, became an outdoors fanatic, and even tried to grow my hair long, though my conservative dad always made me cut it.

Throughout my high school years I wanted to be a psychologist. From high school to college, I was greatly into theater and acting. Acting, like my eccentric mannerisms in the past, and writing in later years, became a way to channel my dreams and desires in a productive way. I was in a few school plays, but I felt like an arrow trapped by its bow, unable to fly out to its full destiny.

By the end of my college freshman year, I knew I wanted to be a writer. I had kept a few journals throughout my teen years, but one night I had a great vision that I was destined to be a great writer like Charles Dickens or Mark Twain. I knew that was my purpose and talent in life: to translate my inner vivid impressions, my 100-frames-per-second runaway imagination, into Romantic literature, poetry, or creative journalism. I was going to leave my mark in this world, to influence people's lives and make them think. I saw my life as a shooting star and believed there would never be another one like me. It was the summer of '82 and at nineteen, with my new fire-filled dream, I felt like I owned the world. I began filling journals with my everyday ventures and thoughts, my own poetry, and passages and ideas from novels. I filled pages with my own philosophical ideas about life and wrote a play based on who I wanted to be. I also became a voracious reader and began drinking alcohol—mostly beer—like it was going out of style.

I believed that as a writer I had to experience everything at least once and live every day with great style, like Napoleon, Hemingway, or my brother Steve. Drinking to me was a part of that free-spirit life, and I did it every chance I could, without reserve.

To stimulate my confidence even more, I began to believe I was a genius. To quote another of my musical idols, John Lennon, I thought, "If there is such a thing as a genius I am one, and if there isn't I don't care." I could intuitively see spiritual forces that others didn't seem to see. Perhaps I had been learning-disabled and was slow in ways, but if you set your heart and mind on a goal like I did, nothing can stop you from success in your own eyes, despite circumstances you have little or no control over. You aren't teachable and maturable unless you believe yourself to be, and will it. Schools and teachers offer knowledge, skills, and guidance; it's up to you to take the initiative, open yourself up and apply it to create who and what you believe you are best meant to be.

I became the arts and entertainment editor for my college newspaper and had a lot of authority, writing and assigning articles for the pages I designed. In my senior year I also became president of the German club.

Many a day I would wander the ivy-covered gothic area around Yale University, journal in hand, pretending to be Hemingway in Paris working on his novels. I would write about Connecticut and experiences based on my life and family, the way Hemingway did about Europe in the roaring twenties or Mark Twain did about life on the Mississippi. I fancied how high school and college students would read their assigned classics, which I had written, for their English classes. I pictured my name on the shelves between F. Scott Fitzgerald and John Steinbeck. Gifted students and professors would discuss and admire my life and works in years ahead, over coffee.

Perhaps unconsciously I was trying to make up for my lost autistic years. Perhaps, you think, the dream bubble was re-emerging. But I didn't feel conceited, and I was very practical. I still believe the road of experience leads to the palace of wisdom. As you can plainly see, I felt pretty much in my prime. Even close friends and girls were entering the picture.

Although I never became a professional reporter or free-lance writer, as was my goal, I did have two articles published in two local Connecticut newspapers. I also had three of my poems published, one of them winning an award. I privately published my own volume of poetry and wrote a book on my family's history, in the literary biography style. I like to think of it as a basis of or internship for my first novel or perhaps book of nonfiction.

During my four years at college I went home to my parents most weekends, since it was a local school, and there weren't many weekend activities. So even though I got a taste for liberal campus life and the real world, I never became fully independent for more than two weeks at a time.

When I went on a summer student-exchange program to Poland after graduation, I was on my own for almost two months, except that everything was organized and there were guides to fall back on if the going got tough. But I was now learning fast to adjust to sudden, unpredictable, illogical changes—something I remember not being able to deal with easily when I was autistic. Again, it really comes down to a choice of self-determination.

In the summer of '86, not having found a job, I decided to push myself to the limits and travel through Europe on my own for a full two months—no one to depend on but God and myself. This was my first real test to prove I could be successful in anything I set my mind to. In school you train yourself for your chosen career and acquire knowledge to enlighten the intellect or stimulate your social life. In travel you acquire knowledge and wisdom through intensified experience to enlighten the soul.

It was the first venture in my life which I had saved for, planned, and organized completely on my own. It was first a test of survival, part of the initiation from college boy to manhood (I was still following in my brother's footsteps); second, a self-imposed internship to train myself for a possible career in travel writing; third, a vacation. One dream at that time was to write a practical, insightful travel book, based on my experiences in Europe, with the intention of making mistakes that future travelers could learn from. I did get to meet the Pope in Rome and paint my name on the former Berlin Wall.

If public schooling was my preparation for the world after Ives and autism, then college and Europe were the entrance exam. Moving to Orlando to become independent, successful in my career, and active in my church and in my personal life is then the intense education of life, while the future of marrying and raising a family in the image of the Lord is the final exam. Getting into heaven is graduation.

I am very much interested in girls—I've had crushes since I was twelve. I did have a girlfriend in my senior year of high school, whom I dated through college when we were home on vacation. Annie was ambitious and highly intelligent and went to law school in Boston. I would take her out dancing; she encouraged me a lot as a writer. And there were others through college.

Much later in Europe I met an Iranian girl, Sima, on a train, and we spent the day in Amsterdam. We became pen pals (she lived in Germany), and I visited her at her brother's place in Los Angeles the following year. I was more serious with her than I was with other girls, and even asked her to marry me, but distance and different backgrounds hampered our relationship.

Finally, after living in Florida a few years, I met Gloria at my church—the beautiful "Angel Eyes" of my dreams whom I got engaged to. We are no longer engaged, but we are working hard on our relationship and both believe we are divinely meant for each other. It is also currently a long-distance relationship. Gloria is a psychology major in school with a goal of becoming a counselor. Like me she is also a writer.

And of course I can't forget Margot, whom I met at culinary school. We have been best friends here in Orlando for the past five years. I was first in love with her, like I had been with hundreds of girls in my lifetime, but now we are just good friends. I have probably gone on more dates with her than with all the others combined. I have been sexually active with girls in the past, but none of them the girlfriends I just mentioned. I was intimate with the loves of my life, but sex never entered the picture. It's weird, but during my college years I always thought sex would ruin our relationship and trust, so I felt more comfortable and free finding girls I hardly knew and cared about to get my kicks with. No emotional strings attached. Just a good time and go our merry way.

While living at college with my roommates, and later on with one of my wild friends, there were many nights of spontaneous parties, bar-hopping, and of course lots of drinking. Ending up with a girl—any girl who was good-looking and willing, regardless of her personality—was usually the end of the means. And it wasn't only fun, but a sort of initiation from boyhood to manhood. Also, I felt that sex gave me a greater air of confidence in relating to women, like the proudness one might feel reaching the top of a high mountain, rather than just admiring it from below.

But lo and behold! I found out that this is really only psychological deception because of our passionate human nature. What I am about to conclude my testimony with tops off everything else in terms of life's worth, and may just blow your mind.

While at culinary school in Rhode Island, I joined the student Christian club and gave my life to Jesus Christ as my personal Lord and Savior, becoming what Jesus himself called a "born-again" Christian. All it means is that you believe that Jesus died for your sins, that you are a lost sinner without Him, and believe He is your only door into heaven, the Lord and your only guiding light. (The Bible also says there is a real hell for those who don't conform their lives to Him.) You are thus born into the eternal kingdom of God. At that point the Holy Spirit resides and manifests itself in your heart and spirit, enabling you to live out the rest of your days by this faith.

My intention here is not to preach but to share the truth that set me free, so that it may also set you free. Christianity is not a manmade religion but the only universal truth from God to anyone, like you and me, who is willing to heed the calling and serve the King by serving others. The choice is ours and the time is now.

I don't regret anything I've experienced (sex, drinking, living on the edge) because I've learned from it. But knowing by faith that God has a wife chosen for me, I no longer believe in sex before marriage, although I still struggle with it. I'm sure many people need to learn and experience lessons for themselves like I did, and that's fine. Sometimes you need to go through black to appreciate white. Also, let me say that I've learned sex will be much more fulfilling with the woman God will give me because we will really care about each other, and we will be comfortable because our emotions will be stable. I have been successful in all my dreams, but then success is only giving everything with what we have, by what we feel in our heart. And no one is excused, not even the once-autistic.

Appendix B
THE AUTISTIC ADULT
AS SEEN
IN *RAIN MAN*

In the film *Rain Man*, Charlie Babbitt, played by Tom Cruise, at one point explains to a nurse that his older brother Raymond, played by Dustin Hoffman, is autistic. The nurse's bewildered reply is "Artistic?" That scene, as silly as it seems, in fact quite realistically portrays what is played out for real, over and over again, every day. For a long time, and even now, to say "autistic" has been to invite a blank or quizzical stare in response.

The unusual achievement of *Rain Man* has been to convey to the general public for the first time a realistic portrait of autism. By virtue of the considerable publicity surrounding the movie and Hoffman's receipt of an Academy Award for his portrayal of Raymond, the public has been shown what autism, or at least one type of autism, looks like, and there now seems to be more of a public awareness of the disability, if not always a true understanding of it. One cable television reporter, Stuart Matringa, went so far as to say of the movie, "Until *Rain Man*, autism was the lunatic locked in the attic of psychology. What *Rain Man* has done is [to have] made autism 'in.' " But the effect has gone further than mere topicality in the entertainment news. By publicizing autism, the film has allowed many people to face and accept autistic people in their own families and communities. One mother of an autistic child wrote to Hoffman that her mother, after seeing *Rain Man*, was able for the first time to discuss her autistic grandson with her friends.

The film tells the story of Charlie Babbitt, a fast-talking, opportunistic car dealer, and his forty-year-old brother, Raymond, who is autistic. When Charlie's millionaire father dies, he leaves only a 1949 Buick Roadmaster convertible to Charlie and three million dollars to an anonymous heir. A furious Charlie, who was counting on the money, discovers that the heir is his hitherto unknown older brother, who lives in a private institution, Wallbrook. The thematic core of the movie is the gradual transformation of Charlie into a caring, though still slightly frustrated, brother to Raymond, and the slight moderation of Raymond's symptoms brought on by his new relationship with Charlie.

Scene by scene, the film skillfully outlines the nature of the disorder. Although Raymond is a savant and not a typical autistic person, he does exhibit the main traits of autism: inability to deal with abstract ideas or reason logically; abnormality in speech (articulate-but-odd, limited, echolalic); absence of eye contact; stiffness in posture and body movement; compulsive gestures; fascination with repetitive movement; overwhelming anxiety communicated through posture; hair-triggered tantrums; and the need for sameness and structure.

Throughout the first part of the film, Charlie and the audience, bit by bit, begin to see the dimensions of Raymond's condition. His imperviousness and rigidity come through in his monotonal recitation of a barrage of statistics on the Roadmaster convertible, his stubborn insistence that he drove the car "only on Mondays," and his inability to participate in "normal" conversational give-and-take. In one scene, Charlie encounters Raymond's extreme obsession with structure when Charlie takes down a book from Raymond's neat, book-laden shelves and Raymond erupts, screaming and hitting himself, then calling pleadingly to the attendant for help. Raymond's need for structure is typical of an autistic person, and is also reflected in his absolute insistence, to the point of frenzy, on seeing "Wapner" at four o'clock every afternoon and his extreme anxiety when he thinks he will miss it.

The film also shows the frightening side of autistic behavior. In a scene in the bathroom of a motel, Charlie innocently turns on the hot water for Raymond's bath. Seeing the steaming water, Raymond goes into a frenzy, screaming appallingly, repeatedly hitting himself out of uncontrollable, overwhelming terror, crying, "*Burn* baby! *Burn* baby!" The cause turns out to be his horrifying memory of accidentally scalding Charlie when Charlie was a baby.

The frustration that relatives of autistic people experience is brought out well. As Charlie slowly develops from a selfish manipulator into an affectionate brother who wants to be emotionally closer to Raymond, he is blocked by Ray's imperviousness and emotional distance. In one scene, Charlie, exasperated, shakes Raymond, crying desperately, "You must be in there somewhere!"

The film never allows the audience to think of Raymond merely as a damaged automaton. It goes to considerable effort to show his humanity, which is there despite his disability. In fact what convinced Dustin Hoffman to make *Rain Man* was a "60 Minutes" segment on idiot savants. "What was most moving to me," says Hoffman, "was the personality that was coming through despite the affliction. They had so many subtle ways of expressing themselves." Hoffman's challenge in the movie was to try to make the revelation of Raymond's humanity convincing.

One of the most moving scenes occurs in the bathroom while Raymond is brushing his teeth. As he looks at himself in the mirror, he says, "Funny rain man." Charlie then realizes that his childhood imaginary companion, his "rain man", is in fact Raymond. Somewhere in the sequence of Charlie's questions and Raymond's abbreviated answers, Raymond leans over and pats Charlie on the head, experimentally and tentatively.

Dustin Hoffman endows this gesture with supreme delicacy. The moment is significant: Raymond has broken through a part of his emotional isolation to some awareness of Charlie as his brother.

The optimism of the film is guarded, however. In one of the final scenes of *Rain Man*, the psychologist asks Raymond, "Do you want to stay with Charlie Babbitt or go back to Wallbrook?" Raymond at first answers, "Yeah, stay with Charlie Babbitt." To the repeated question, he then answers, "Yeah, stay with Charlie Babbitt, go back to Wallbrook." "Stop! Stop!" Charlie cries. "Enough. There's no need to humiliate him further." He leans over and puts his hand comfortingly on Raymond's arm and says, "It's all right, Ray. It's all right." Charlie leans his head on Ray's shoulder and Raymond, in a brief display of emotional connection, leans his head on Charlie's, while Charlie says, "I *like* having you for my big brother, Ray."

Two years of research went into *Rain Man*. The most important concern of those involved, according to Gail Mutrux, the associate producer, was that the script depict the autistic adult accurately, capable of only minor adjustments and unchanging in the main characteristics of the disability. Three directors quit *Rain Man* in the early stages of production largely out of frustration over the limitations placed on the character of Raymond by the insistence on realism in the portrayal of his autism. Each in essence found himself asking Hoffman, "You don't look at people? You don't talk? How can there be a story or a movie?"

The writers, producers, directors, and Hoffman himself all used a number of consultants for the film and visited a number of facilities for autistic persons. The principal consultant was Dr. Bernard Rimland, director of the Institute for Child Behavior Research in San Diego, California. Another was Dr. Ruth Sullivan, director of the Autism Services Center. (Both Dr. Rimland and Dr.

Sullivan have autistic children who served as models for the character of Raymond.) Other consultants were Dr. Bodel Silverstein, a behavior therapist; Dr. Darold Treffert, a specialist on idiot savants; and Dr. Peter Tanguay, a child psychiatrist on the staff of the UCLA Neuropsychiatric Institute.

The original screenplay modeled Raymond on a real mentally retarded savant named Kim, who had an unlimited ability to recall facts and figures. Hoffman met with Kim and adopted the way Kim moved and walked for the character of Raymond. In addition, Hoffman met with and used his observations on three other autistic savants—Mark Rimland, David Parsons, and Peter Guthrie—to create Raymond. Peter Guthrie was especially helpful because he had an active relationship with his "normal" brother, Kevin. Hoffman and Cruise spent time bowling with Peter and Kevin in order to observe the nuances in the interaction between the two brothers. From Peter, Hoffman acquired the nasal, monotone voice, the habit of spelling out names, and the obsession with statistics.

(The exposure to the actors playing an autistic man and his brother had an interesting reciprocal effect on Peter and Kevin. Two weeks after that first meeting, Kevin received a telephone call from Peter. When Kevin asked him what he wanted, Peter replied, "I just wanted to talk to you, K-E-V-I-N." Never in their twenty-five years together, said Kevin, had Peter ever said anything remotely like that.)

Dustin Hoffman also prepared for his role by visiting several facilities, including a sheltered workshop, the Devereaux School in Santa Barbara, and L'Arc Ranch in Los Angeles County. Mutrux, who did a great deal of the research for Hoffman, visited other workshops and schools and taped interviews with a variety of authorities in different fields, that affect the lives of autistic people. Hoffman studied *A Portrait of an Autistic Young Man*, a film about Joseph Sullivan, Dr. Ruth Sullivan's son, and met with Temple Grandin, in her own words, a "recovering" autistic and author of the autobiography *Emergence: Labeled Autistic*, to discuss the complexities of the disability.

The last scene of *Rain Man* shows Raymond on the train sitting beside the director of Wallbrook. As the train slowly pulls away from the station, he stares impassively ahead, oblivious of Charlie, who is standing, waving, on the platform. Raymond is heading back to Wallbrook and an institutional life. Though dramatically effective, this ending is probably not entirely realistic in view of the opportunities now available for autistic people. The trend now is to take developmentally disabled people out of institutions and place them in group homes or supervised apartments and have them work in supervised workshops or a job in the community. There is improved education for the handicapped and a multiplicity of private and public programs to help people like Raymond acquire a degree of self-sufficiency. If Raymond had been a real person today, he almost certainly would not have gone back to Wallbrook. Most realistically, he might have entered a group home or a social-worker-supported condominium. And since he was high functioning, he could have held a job in the community.

Several other endings were in fact considered for *Rain Man*: One would have shown Charlie and Ray at a Dodgers game; another had Raymond and Charlie fishing together; a third, the most realistic perhaps, would have had Raymond stay with Charlie and go into a group home. But this was rejected because it would have in essence been the start of a new story. Rumor has it that a sequel to *Rain Man* may be in the planning stages now, which is a testament to the honesty and power of this movie, and the interest and sympathy it generated in viewers. For many, it was a first introduction to autism, and helped to make this baffling condition less strange and fearsome to those who know little about it.

So for dramatic purposes in the movie Raymond goes back

to Wallbrook. This may not have been the most realistic, but it avoided false optimism about Raymond's ability to improve, and it almost certainly was the best ending for conveying to the audience the basic truth about autism: The autistic person, despite the moderation of deficits and sometimes even dramatic improvements, never loses the inherent characteristics of autism.

Appendix C
SUMMARY CHART:
PRESCHOOL THROUGH HIGH SCHOOL

	TOM	JIMMY*	POLLY	BILL
Original diagnosis:	Atypical personality disorder	Autistic symptoms; emotionally disturbed	Personality disturbance/autistic tendencies	Atypical personality with autistic features
Referred by:	Clinic pediatrician	Clinic pediatrician	Clinic nursery school teacher	Public school kindergarten teacher
Reason for referral:	Clinging; bland; slow in all developmental landmarks; limited, whispered speech	Aggressive behavior; no speech; hyperactive; tantrums; self-involved	Wild, violent behavior; anxiety; panics easily	Bizarre behavior; limited speech; babbling, meaningless shouts; a loner
Strengths:	Determination; cooperative; available to teaching	Aware of people and surroundings; motivated and quick to learn; "charm"; sense of humor	Learns quickly; wants to relate; normal speech; determination	Accessible to teaching; cooperative; interested in dramatics; literary ability
Weaknesses:	Remoteness; echolalic speech; very stubborn	Poor vision and motor development; physically violent (biting, pinching, etc.)	Unpredictable emotionally; can be unreachable"	Distanced emotionally; rigid; panics easily
Education:	Preschool; public school special education through high school; vocational and summer camp	Preschool, 2 years; residential school, 5 years; program for communication disorders until "graduation"	Nursery school, 1 year; clinic nursery school, 1 year; preschool public education program for emotionally disturbed (changed to program for mentally retarded), 1 year; high school vocational program in special education high school; camp for mentally retarded, 4 years	Preschool, 3 years; phased back to public school; college, 4 years; culinary institute, 2 years

*Refused permission for testing   **Deceased   ***Mother unable to be present for Vineland

DAVID	KAREN	JOHN	LARRY**	ERIC***
Aphasia; mildly retarded	Atypical development with autistic behavior	Neurologically impaired; emotionally disturbed	Emotionally disturbed; autistic psychotic features	Congenital autism
Clinic pediatrician	Clinic pediatrician	Clinic pediatrician	Clinic psychiatrist	Clinic pediatrician
Delay in speech and all developmental landmarks; placement to be diagnostic	Lacks speech— had only 3 words; remote; does not respond to people; high anxiety; fearful	Hyperactivity; impulsivity; "easily disoriented and hysterical"	Wild, uncontrolled behavior; "severe emotional problems"; speech often unrelated and rapid, i.e., "shot-gun"	Lack of speech; "out of touch"; "unreachable"; repetitive behaviors; tantrums
Determination; cooperative; wants to relate though handicapped by disability	Wants to relate; some speech; available to teaching; remarkable memory	Very verbal; beguiling; relates well superficially; good singer	Intelligent response to one-on-one treatment; appealing and attractive appearance	Apparent friendliness that has no reality—"like grabbing mist"
Distanced emotionally; talks in a whisper; limited speech	Repetitive; echolalic; fearful; "often unreachable"	Distractable; explosive	Immature motor and verbal development; echolalic; swearing	Inaccessible to teaching; rigid; anxious
Preschool; public school special education communication disorders program; special education camp	Preschool, 1 year; private special education school, 7 years; private special school; two residential schools graduated from second)	Normal nursery school; preschool, 3 years; private special school, 8 years; boarding school, 1¾ years; special education high school	Preschool; residential treatment center; communication disorders program; summer special education camp	Preschool, 1 year; Moslenn school, 1 year; special education through high school, communication disorders program

Appendix D
SUMMARY CHART: ADULT OUTCOMES
Testing Date: Oct.–Nov., 1987

	I. Q. SCORES			VINELAND SCORES			
	VERBAL	PERFOR-MANCE	FULL SCALE	COMMU-NICA-TION	DAILY LIVING	SOCIAL-IZATION	ADAPTIVE BEHAVIOR COMPOSITE
TOM 27 years old	64	69	65	38	80	83	62
JIMMY not tested; parent refused permission	–	–	–	–	–	–	–
POLLY 28 years old	63	62	61	36	85	59	55
BILL 24 years old	103	95	94	97	108	74	90
DAVID 22 years old	70	69	69	45	57	49	47
KAREN 25 years old	62	52	55	20	49	44	34
JOHN 26 years old	73	65	68	65	119	111	92
LARRY deceased	–	–	–	–	–	–	–
ERIC 22 years old	51	51	46	–	–	–	–

ABC	CURRENT LIVING SITUATION	CURRENT OCCUPATION	DEGREE MENTAL RETARDA- TION
107 quite autistic	at home; on list for group home or apartment	dishwasher at restaurant	mild
——	at home	sheltered workshop	moderate
49 probably not autistic, more atypical	supervised apartment; shares with another handicapped woman	sales department at discount store	moderate
63 possibly autistic	own apartment, car	operates computerized ordering of supplies for restaurant	none
78 probably autistic	at home	back room loader, discount store	mild
126 autistic	supervised apartment; shares with a friend	fast-food restaurant	moderate
52 possibly autistic	shares a condominium with another handicapped man	volunteer at nursing home	mild
——	——	——	——
101 probably autistic	at home	sheltered workshop	severe

GLOSSARY

Affect. How a person feels at a particular time. Anger, sadness, elation, and depression are all examples of affects. Another word for affect is mood. The type of affect, its appropriateness to the situation, and its persistence are important patterns that help determine a diagnosis. Affect can be a symptom, a sign, or a disorder.

Aphasia. Impairment or loss of the faculty of using or understanding spoken or written language.

Asperger's syndrome. Those children who are poorly coordinated in a movement and have circumscribed "intellectual interests" fit the picture of Asperger's syndrome.

Atypical personality disorder. *See* Pervasive personality disorder.

Auditory integration training. Known as AIT, this is an emerging treatment for disorders of auditory processing. It was popularized through Annabel Stehli's book, *The Sound of a Miracle*, which described her autistic daughter's improvement through this treatment.

Autism. A severely incapacitating, usually lifelong, developmental disability. It begins at birth or during the first three years of life. It is three times more common in males than females and has been found throughout the world in families of all racial, ethnic, social, and economic backgrounds. It is marked by slow development of physical, social, and learning skills. Inability to relate to others is its hallmark.

Autistic savant. An autistic with usually one extraordinary ability in memory, music, art, or math—for example, to remember the numbers of all the exits on the highways in a state or to do complicated mathematical problems.

Community house. An organization within a town that offers a variety of services to the local community, e.g., day care for senior citizens or workshop training for the handicapped.

Concrete thinking. To take words literally, to attach limited meaning to words. An inability to think in abstractions.

Echolalia. Repetition of words or phrases spoken by another.

Facilitated communication. Developed in Australia, it is a system of teaching nonverbal children to type answers to questions on a typewriter or computer with the help of an adult "facilitator." The facilitator assists the child by placing a hand gently on the child's hand, back, or shoulders, but does not guide the child's answers.

Fine motor skills. The ability to use the small muscles of the body, such as those in the hands, feet, fingers, and toes.

Fragile-X syndrome. A genetic condition in males in which one part of the X-chromosome has a defect. The condition causes mental retardation and many behavioral and cognitive disabilities. Fragile-X males typically have long faces and very large ears and testicles.

Gross motor skills. The ability to use the large muscles of the body.

Kanner's syndrome. In 1943, Dr. Leo Kanner, a psychiatrist, was the first to describe an abnormal behavior pattern seen in young children that he described as *early infantile autism*, now known as Kanner's syndrome. This behavior pattern starts within the first thirty months of life and is distinguished by inability to form normal social relationships, abnormal development of speech or lack of speech, and avoidance of eye contact.

Labile. Unstable.

Mainstreaming. The practice of putting a handicapped child in regular school classes for certain, sometimes all, subjects.

Neuromotor. Physical movement controlled by the nervous system, i.e., cutting with scissors, walking, running.

Obsessive. Completely possessed by one idea.

Perseveration. Extremely repetitive movement or speech. This is thought to be a creation of a person's own inner preoccupations and is a frequent characteristic of autistics.

Pervasive development disorder. Formerly known as atypical personality disorder, PDD is characterized by lack of responsiveness to others, resistance to change, oddities of movement, severe disturbance in social relations, abnormalities of language development, distortion in the development of affects, and vulnerability to unusually high levels of anxiety. This is a diagnostic classification used within the syndrome of autism.

PET scans. Positron emission tomography. A technology that permits measurement of the metabolic areas of the brain.

Psychogenic. Having its origin in the mind or in a mental condition or process.

Psychosis. Any mental derangement or abnormality existing at any one moment.

Psychotic. Mentally ill, unstable, out-of-touch with reality. Characterized by amoral, antisocial behavior, inability to form meaningful relationships or to learn from experience.

Schizophrenia. A mental disorder with teenage onset, associated with lack of motivation, social withdrawal, emotional flattening, hallucinations, and delusions. Not related to autism.

Supported employment. Paid employment of handicapped or developmentally disabled persons, usually supervised by a job coach.

Symbiotic personality type. A personality type that clings to another (mother, teacher, etc.) almost to the point of union.

FOR MORE INFORMATION
ABOUT AUTISM

These are national organizations that provide varied services to parents of children with autism, and to autistics themselves. For more information call or write to request a copy of their newsletter or other publications. Organizations or branches of organizations also thrive at the state, county, or local level. Consult the yellow pages of your telephone directory or your library or local mental health association for these groups.

American Association of
University Affiliated Programs
for Persons with Developmental
Disabilities (AAUAP)
8630 Fenton St., Suite 410
Silver Spring, MD 20910
Tel: 301-588-8252

The ARC
500 East Border St.
Suite 300
Arlington, TX 76010
Tel: 817-261-6003

The Association for Persons with
Severe Handicaps (TASH)
Tel: 410-828-8274

Autism Research Institute
(formerly Institute for Child
Behavior Research)
4182 Adams Ave.
San Diego, CA 92116
Tel: 619-281-7165
Contact: Bernard Rimland,
Ph.D., Director

Autism Services Center
Hotline
Prichard Building
605 9th St.
P.O. Box 507
Huntington, WV 25710
Tel: 304-525-8014
Contact: Ruth Sullivan, Ph.D.

Autism Society of America
National Office
7910 Woodmont Ave., Suite 650
Bethesda, MD 20814
Tel: 301-657-0881

Autism Training Center
Old Main 316
Marshall University
Huntington, WV 25755
Tel: 304-696-2332

Fragile X Foundation
1441 York St., Suite 303
Denver, CO 80206
Tel: 303-333-6155
David Nommenson, Director

International Rett Syndrome
Association
9121 Piscataway Rd.
Suite 2B
Clinton, MD 20735
Tel: 301-856-3334

Joseph P. Kennedy, Jr.,
Foundation
1325 G St., N.W., Suite 50
Washington, D.C. 20005
Tel: 202-393-1250

Kids on the Block
9385 C Gerwig Lane
Columbia, MD 21406
Tel: 410-290-9095;
800-368-KIDS

National Organization on
Disability (NOD)
910 16th St., N.W., Suite 600

Washington, D.C. 20006
Tel: 202-293-5960

National Rehabilitation
Information Center
4407 Eighth St., N.E.
Washington, D.C. 20017
Tel: 301-588-9284

Parent Educational Advocacy
Training Center
228 Pitt St., Suite 300
Alexandria, VA
Tel: 703-691-7826

Parents Education and Assistance
for Kids
6055 Lehman Drive, Suite 101
Colorado Springs, CO 80918
Tel: 303-531-9400
Contact: Judy Martz and
Barbara Buswell, Directors

Rehabilitation Research and
Training Center
Virginia Commonwealth
University
1314 W. Main St.
Richmond, VA 23284-0001
Tel: 804-828-1851

Sibling Information Network
62 Washington St.
Middletown, CT 06457-2844
Tel: 203-344-7500
or
Dept. of Educational Psychology
Box U-64
University of Connecticut

Storrs, CT 06268
Tel: 203-486-4031

Siblings for Significant Change
105 E. 22nd St.
New York, NY 10010
Tel: 212-420-0430

Special Olympics
1325 G St., N.W.
Suite 500
Washington, D.C. 20005
Tel: 202-628-3630

TEACCH
(Treatment and Education of
Autistic and Related
Communication Handicapped
Children and Adults)
Division TEACCH, CB #7180
Medical School Wing E
Chapel Hill, NC 27599–7180
Tel: 919-966-2174
Contact: Eric Schopler, Ph.D.,
Director

Technical Assistance for Parent
Programs (TAPP)
95 Berkeley St.
Boston, MA 02116

Contact: Martha Ziegler,
Director
Tel: 617-482-2915

The following addresses are
TAPP regional centers.

Parent Information Center
151-A Manchester St.
P.O. Box 1422
Concord, NH 03301
Tel: 603-224-6299
Contact: Judith Raskin, Director

PACER CENTER
Parent Advocacy Coalition for
Educational Rights
4826 Chicago Ave., South
Minneapolis, MN 55417-1098
Tel: 800-53-PACER (MN only)
612-827-2966
Contact: Marge Goldberg or
Paula Goldberg, Directors

Georgia/ARC
Parents Educating Parents
2860 East Point St., Suite 200
East Point, GA 30344
Tel: 404-761-2745
Contact: Tom Query, Executive
Director

BIBLIOGRAPHY

Ames, Louise Bates. *Arnold Gesell, Themes of His Work*. New York: Human Sciences Press, 1989.

Arnstein, Helene S. "An Approach to the Severely Disturbed Child." In *Some Approaches to Teaching Autistic Children*, edited by P.T.B. Weston. London: Pergamon Press. 1965.

Associated Press. "Real Rain Man Thrives with Film." *New Haven (Conn.) Register*, Feb. 19, 1989, A2.

Axline, Virginia Mae. *Play Therapy; The Inner Dynamics of Childhood*. Cambridge: Houghton Mifflin Co., 1947.

Barsch, Ray H. *Achieving Perceptual Motor Efficiency. A Perceptual Motor Curriculum*, vol. I. Seattle: Special Child Publications, 1967.

Bender, L. "Childhood Schizophrenia: A Clinical Study of 100 Schizophrenic Children." *American Journal of Orthopsychiatry* 17 (1947): 40–56.

———. "Schizophrenia in Childhood: Its Recognition, Description and Treatment." *American Journal of Orthopsychiatry* 26(3) (1956): 499–506.

Bettelheim, Bruno. *Love Is Not Enough*. Glencoe, Ill.: The Free Press,1950.

Caparulo, B.K., and Cohen, D.J. "Developmental language disorders in the neuropsychiatric disorders of childhood." In *Children's Language*, edited by K.E. Nelson. New York: Gardner Press, 1983.

Cohen, Donald J., and Donnellan, Ann M., eds. *Handbook of Autism and Pervasive Developmental Disorders*. New York: John Wiley & Sons, 1987.

Cohen, D.J., Caparulo, B.K., Shaguritz, B.A. and Bowers, M.B.J. "Dopamine and serotinin metabolism in neuropsychiatrically disturbed children: CSF homovanillic acid and 5-hydroxyindolacetic acid." *Archives of General Psychiatry* 34 (1977): 545–50.

Cruickshank, William M., Bentzen, Frances A., Ratzenburg, Frederick H., and Tannhauser, Miriam T. *A Teaching Method for Brain-Injured and Hyperactive Children: A Demonstration Pilot Study.* Syracuse, N.Y.: Syracuse University Press, 1961.

Cutler, Barbara C., and Kozloff, Martin A. "Living with Autism: Effects on Family Needs." In *Handbook of Autism and Pervasive Developmental Disorders*, edited by D.J. Cohen and A.M. Donnellan. New York: John Wiley & Sons, 1987.

Dahl, E.K., Cohen, D.J., and Provence, S. "Developmental disorders evaluated in early childhood: Clinical and multivariate approaches to nosology of PDD." *Journal of the American Academy of Child Psychiatry* 25 (1986): 170–80.

Despert, L. "Some Considerations Relating to the Genesis of Autistic Behavior in Children." *American Journal of Orthopsychiatry* 21 (1951): 335–50.

Elgar, Sybil. "Teaching Autistic Children." In *Early Childhood Autism*, edited by J.K. Wing. London: Pergamon Press, 1966.

Grandin, Temple, and Scariano, Margaret. *Emergence, Labeled Autistic.* Novato, Calif.: Arena Press, 1986.

Kanner, L. "Autistic Disturbances of Affective Contact." *Nervous Child* 2 (1943): 217–50.

————. "Follow-up of eleven autistic children originally reported in 1943." *Journal of Autism and Childhood Schizophrenia* 1(2) (1971): 119–45.

Kephart, Newell C. *The Slow Learner in the Classroom.* Columbus, Ohio: Charles E. Merrill, 1960.

Lieberman, Dawn A., and Malone, Mary Bonyai. *Sexuality and Social Awareness.* Yalesville, Conn.: Benhaven Press, n.d.

Mahler, M. "On childhood psychosis and schizophrenia: Autistic and symbiotic infantile psychoses." In *Psychoanalytic Study of the Child*, vol. 7. New York: International Universities Press, 1952.

————. *Our Human Symbioses and the Vicissitudes of Individuation.* New York: International Universities Press, 1968.

Marcus, Lee M. and Shopler, Eric. "Working with Families: A Developmental Perspective." In *Handbook of Autism and Pervasive Developmental Disorders*, edited by D.J. Cohen and A.M. Donnellan. New York: John Wiley & Sons, 1987.

Matringa, Stuart. "Night of the Rain Men." *Cable TV Guide*, Feb. 1990, 18–23.

Provence, S., and Dahl, E. K. "Disorders of Atypical Development: Diagnostic Issues Raised by a Spectrum Disorder." In *Handbook of Autism and Pervasive Developmental Disorders*, edited by D.J. Cohen and A.M. Donnellan. New York: John Wiley & Sons, 1987.

Putnam, M.G., Rank, B., Pavenstedt, E., Anderson, E.N., and Rawson, I. "Round Table, 1974, Case Study of an A-Typical Two-and-a-Half-Year-Old." *American Journal of Orthopsychiatry* 18 (1948): 1–30.

Putnam, M.G., Rank, B., and Kaplan, S. "Notes on John I.: A case of primal depression in an infant." In *Psychoanalytic Study of the Child*, vol. 6. New York: International Universities Press, 1951.

Rank, B. "Intensive Study and Treatment of Pre-School Children Who Show Marked Personality Deviations of 'A-Typical Development' and Their Parents." In *Emotional Problems of Early Childhood*. New York: Basic Books, 1955.

Reilly, Sue, "A Welcome Rain." *New Haven (Conn.) Register*, Jan. 30, 1989, 17–19.

Riddle, Mark, "Individual and Parental Psychotherapy in Autism." In *Handbook of Autism and Pervasive Developmental Disorders*, edited by D.J. Cohen and A.M. Donnellan. New York: John Wiley & Sons, 1987.

Ritvo, S., and Provence, S. "Form perception and imitation in some autistic children: Diagnostic findings and their contextual interpretation." In *Psychoanalytic Study of the Child*. vol. 8. New York: International Universities Press, 1953.

Sparrow, S., Rescorlo, L.A., Provence, S., Condon, S., Goudreau, D., and Cicchetti, D. "Mild atypical children—preschool and follow-up." *Journal of the American Academy of Child Psychiatry* 26 (1986): 181–85.

Volkmar, F.R., "Autism and Pervasive Development Disorders." In *Child and Adolescent Psychiatry: A Comprehensive Textbook*, edited by M. Lewis. Baltimore: Williams and Wilkinson, 1991.

————. "Social Development." In *Handbook of Autism and Pervasive Developmental Disorders*, edited by D.J. Cohen and A.M. Donnellan. New York: John Wiley & Sons, 1987.

Volkmar, F.R., Cicchetti, D., Dykens, E., Sparrow, S., Leckman, J.F., and Cohen, D.J. "An Evaluation of the Autistic Behavior Checklist." *Journal of Autism and Developmental Disorders* 18 (1)(1988): 83.

Volkmar, F.R., Stier, D.M., and Cohen, D.J. "Age of onset of pervasive developmental disorder." *American Journal of Psychiatry* 142 (1985): 1450–52.

Weston, T.B., ed. *Some Approaches to Teaching Autistic Children.* London: Pergamon Press, 1965.

Wing, J.K., ed. *Early Childhood Autism: Clinical, Educational, and Social Aspects.* London: Pergamon Press, 1966.

Wing, L., and Attwood, A. "Syndromes of autism and atypical development." In *Handbook of Autism and Pervasive Developmental Disorders*, edited by D.J. Cohen and A.M. Donnellan. New York: John Wiley & Sons, 1987.

INDEX

Due to the nature of the subject of autism and the case history approach, the same or similar behaviors and conditions occur throughout this book. Therefore, only pages are cited that give fully developed or defined information for each entry. For example, "crying" is indexed only where it is discussed as an aspect of Fragile X syndrome, but not in all instances where children or parents cry from frustration, fear, anger, or relief.

Readers are referred to traits which characterize autism on page 31 and page 190, and to the glossary definition on page 213. The table of contents for the case studies (pages vii–viii) provides guidance to the main concern discussed for each child, and the reactions of or problems faced by the parents.